Niobrara County
High School
Library

WITHDRAWN

ENCYCLOPEDIA OF GOOD HEALTH

EXERCISE

ENCYCLOPEDIA OF GOOD HEALTH

EXERCISE

Series Editors

MARIO ORLANDI, Ph.D., M.P.H.

and

DONALD PRUE, Ph.D.

Text by

ANNETTE SPENCE

Facts On File Publications
New York • Oxford

A FRIEDMAN GROUP BOOK

First published in 1988 by Facts On File Publications, Inc.
460 Park Avenue South
New York, New York 10016

Library of Congress Cataloging-in-Publication Data

Spence, Annette.
Exercise.

(Encyclopedia of good health)
Includes index.
Summary: Provides information on all aspects of exercise, including methods to measure and improve physical fitness.
1. Exercise—Juvenile literature. [1. Exercise. 2. Physical fitness] I. Orlandi, Mario A.
II. Prue, Donald. III. Title. IV. Series: Spence, Annette.
Encyclopedia of good health.
GV481.S649   1988   613.7′1   87-20207
ISBN 0-8160-1671-2

British CIP data available upon request

ENCYCLOPEDIA OF GOOD HEALTH: EXERCISE
was prepared and produced by
Michael Friedman Publishing Group, Inc.
15 West 26th Street
New York, New York 10010

Designer: Rod Gonzalez
Art Director: Mary Moriarty
Illustrations: Kenneth Spengler

Typeset by BPE Graphics, Inc.
Color separated, printed, and bound in Hong Kong by South Seas
International Press Company Ltd.

1 3 5 7 9 10 8 6 4 2

About the Series Editors

Mario Orlandi is chief of the Division of Health Promotion Research of the American Health Foundation. He has a Ph.D. in psychology with further study in health promotion. He has written and edited numerous books and articles, among them The American Health Foundation Guide to Lifespan Health *(Dodd Mead, 1984), and has received numerous grants, awards, and commendations. Orlandi lives in New York City.*

Dr. Donald M. Prue is a management consultant specializing in productivity improvement and wellness programs in business and industrial settings. He was formerly a senior scientist at the American Health Foundation and holds a doctorate in clinical psychology. He has published over forty articles and books on health promotion and was recognized in the Congressional Record *for his work. Prue lives in Houston, Texas.*

About the Author

Annette Spence received a degree in journalism from the University of Tennessee at Knoxville. Her articles have appeared in Redbook, Weight Watchers Magazine, Cosmopolitan, *and* Bride's, *and she has contributed to a number of books. Spence is associate editor for Whittle Communications, a health media company in New York City. She lives in Stamford, Connecticut.*

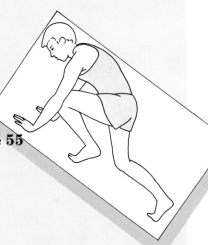

How to Use
This Book

Exercise is part of a six-volume encyclopedia series of books on health topics significant to junior-high students. These health topics are closely related to each other, and for this reason, you'll see references to the other volumes in the series appearing throughout the book. You'll also see references to the other pages *within* this book. These references are important because they tell you where you can find more inter-related and interesting information on the specific subject at hand.

Like each of the books in the series, this book is divided into two sections. The first section tells you why it's a good idea for you to know about this health topic and how it affects you. The second section helps you find ways to improve and maintain your health. We include quizzes and plans designed to help you see how these health issues are relative to you. It's your responsibility to take advantage of them and apply them to your life. Even though this book was written expressly for you and other people your age, you are the one who's in control of learning from it and exercising good health habits for the rest of your life.

What's Important For Me To Know About Exercise?

What do you think of when you think of exercise? Most people think of muscle-bulging weight lifters and pencil-thin fashion models, but that's only what the media has led us to believe fitness is. Exercise is climbing the stairs, walking the dog, hitting a tennis ball, and shoveling snow. Exercise makes you feel great today and keeps you healthier over the years. In this book we won't be dealing with the high-tech weight machines and body-perfect aerobic instructors you see on television and in the magazines. Instead we'll be looking at practical, everyday activities that you probably never thought of as exercise before. Forget about what commercials make us *think* fitness is. What do *you* really need to know about exercise? It's quite simple.

Over 20,000,000 people around the world play basketball. It provides aerobic activity and the excitement of fast-paced team effort.

Exercise Helps You to Feel and Look Good!

In a world of automobiles, escalators, elevators, power lawn mowers, vacuum cleaners, and other convenience devices, it's easy to forget about how great exercise is. Without knowing it, you probably do things every day that are good exercise: phys ed class, marching band practice, baseball games, and Saturday night dances keep you active. At the very least, you're on your feet and moving, which can't always be said about many adults in this country.

The good news, then, is that many junior high school students exercise regularly—without always realizing it. The bad news: Government studies show that kids are in poorer shape than they've ever been. Not only does the American Heart Association report that young people are fatter than they were during the 1960s, the American Academy of Pediatrics recently stated that one-third of the nation's children over the age of twelve have high blood cholesterol levels. What's more, most children have trouble meeting the average fitness standards. Why? After-school television and snacks seem to be more attractive to young people than a neighborhood softball game or raking the lawn. Also, poor eating habits tend to catch up with us as we grow older; a toddler can "burn off" the extra calories he eats faster than a teenager can (see "Nutrition" and "Working Off Extra Weight," page 20).

Considering that exercise does all kinds of great things for the body and the mind, it's really too bad that so many people miss out on it. The role fitness plays in your life—from now until you're a senior citizen—is something to think about. Read on for healthy benefits.

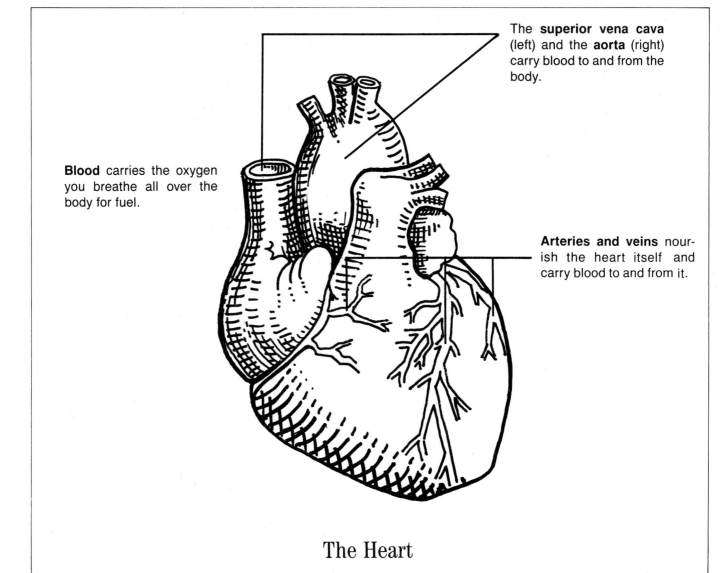

The **superior vena cava** (left) and the **aorta** (right) carry blood to and from the body.

Blood carries the oxygen you breathe all over the body for fuel.

Arteries and veins nourish the heart itself and carry blood to and from it.

The Heart

Muscle Tone

If you stayed in bed for weeks without walking, the muscles in your legs would shrink. Once you did get out of bed, walking would be a nearly impossible task.

Exercise is the only thing that develops muscles—not protein pills or steaks (see "Food for Fitness," page 91). In order to keep our muscles in good working order, exercise is a must. That's not to say we all need Hercules-like biceps. While heavy-duty workouts can help you build a star-quality body, most of us only need a moderate exercise plan to:

- get the heart pumping more blood. This supplies the muscles with more oxygen, which helps them to use energy (or burn calories) faster;
- strengthen and tone muscles. This builds lean tissue, which makes the body look firm instead of pudgy. You may know someone whose body is flabby but who's not really overweight. Even without dieting, regular exercise could help him or her look slimmer. As a matter of fact, people who diet to lose a lot of weight should incorporate exercise into their weight-loss plans, too. Otherwise, they will probably still look flabby, not trim.

Heart Health

Don't ever take your heart for granted. It's an amazing muscle that thrives on exercise. Exercise works the heart harder than when you're sitting. With each stroke it pumps more blood and becomes stronger and thicker. If you exercise regularly, the heart adapts by beating more slowly, squeezing out more and more blood with each pump. That's good, because in the long run, the heart doesn't have to work as hard. By pumping more blood in fewer beats, this powerful muscle:

○ receives more oxygen-containing blood. An increased oxygen supply means the heart is less likely to suffer from an oxygen shortage, which helps cause heart attacks (see ''Nutrition'');
○ increases blood volume throughout all the body's arteries, veins, and capillaries. A healthy heart opens up these passages, helping to prevent high blood pressure and blockages, both of which could lead to strokes or heart attacks;
○ is stronger, so it's able to handle football game tie-breakers, marathons, family moves from one town to another, and other stressful events;
○ makes sure all your muscles get enough blood, so you have more energy and don't tire as quickly.

As surprising as it may seem, heart attacks and high blood pressure are health issues that should concern you. A recent study of 400 high school students showed that nearly half had a heart disease risk factor: high blood pressure, high cholesterol levels, or obesity. A healthy heart is essential (see ''How to Take Your Pulse,'' page 58).

eart Trivia

○ Your heart is about as big as your two fists.
○ Like your other muscles, the heart builds up bulk with exercise. A trained athlete's heart might be 20 percent bigger than one belonging to a nonexerciser.
○ Every day, your heart pumps about 4,300 gallons (16,275 liters) of blood. That's enough to fill about 85 bathtubs!
○ As a person becomes more and more fit and his or her heart rate slows down, the heart pumps even more blood—as much as 25 percent more.
○ The heart pushes blood through about 60,000 miles (97,000 kilometers) of arteries, veins, and capillaries. That's enough to wrap around the earth twice.
○ Fatty-food cholesterol deposits and cigarette smoking can promote blockage of those blood passageways. The first solution, of course, is to eliminate the cause. Exercise offsets the effect (see ''Nutrition'' and ''Substance Abuse'').

Lung Power

What happens when you run four laps around the track? Unless you're a trained athlete, you probably do some huffing and puffing. That's good, as long as you aren't overdoing it (see "Take It Easy!" page 56). When you exercise, the lungs take in more oxygen, increasing their capacity and the amount of oxygen in your blood. Another benefit to a healthier respiratory system is that your stamina is increased. Developing your lung capacity now—being able to breathe in deeply when you're biking up a big hill—will give you an advantage today, as well as when you get older and more prone to health problems (see "Breathe!" page 76).

Bone Strength

Inactivity weakens the bones, and exercise strengthens the bones. In fact, scientists have found that a bone-weakening disease afflicting older women, osteoporosis, may be prevented with exercise that strengthens bones by improving blood flow to bone cells and putting your weight on them (see "Nutrition").

We also know that an active lifestyle increases joint flexibility. By working your joints, you increase their blood flow, which is just like feeding them. Senior citizens who've exercised throughout their lives have an easier time getting around.

Last Week's Workout

Let's evaluate your average week of fitness. On a piece of paper, draw up a chart like the one we have here. Thinking back, try to remember all the big and little activities you performed during the past week (we give you some examples here). Write them in the appropriate space on your paper, then check out your status on the next page.

	SPORTS	RECREATION	WORK	TRAVEL
Mon.	Baseball	Dancing	Shoveled snow Mopped kitchen	Walked to food store
Tues.	Tennis	Roller skating	Painted garage	Biked to choir practice
Wed.	etc.	etc.	etc.	etc.
Thurs.				
Fri.				
Sat.				
Sun.				

Think about all the activity involved in a task as simple as shoveling snow: bending over, shoving the shovel into the snow, lifting the shovel and standing up straight, then lifting the shovel and moving the snow to another location. No wonder this job is considered a vigorous form of exercise!

Joe McNally/Wheeler Pictures

Evaluation

1. Give yourself 10 points for every aerobic activity. Aerobic means "with air": if you breathe hard while doing the exercise and it is (1) performed for twenty or more minutes; (2) keeps you moving without stopping (a twenty-minute game of basketball would qualify, but doubles tennis, a sport that doesn't have you running and hitting the ball every minute, won't); (3) works you reasonably hard, it is an aerobic exercise. (Twenty minutes of dish-washing won't increase your heart rate, but twenty minutes of shoveling snow will.) Consult the "Heart-Smart Aerobics" list on page 33 for help.

2. Give yourself 7 points for every sport that *doesn't* qualify as an aerobic activity. Examples: doubles tennis, baseball, volleyball.

3. Give yourself 5 points for each time you took part in recreation, work, or travel that doesn't qualify as an aerobic activity, but does require a lot of moving, bending, or stretching. Examples: painting the garage, a quick bike ride to choir practice, vacuuming your bedroom.

4. Give yourself 3 points for every activity that wasn't mandatory. Examples: You walked to the food store even though Dad offered to drive you. You offered to sweep the basement. You convinced your friends to play records and dance instead of hanging out at the coffee shop.

5. Give yourself 1 point for every school team event you participated in. Examples: Tennis practice on Tuesday and Thursday gives you 2 points. Monday night's baseball game gives you 1 point.

Scoring

75 points and up: Your typical week is filled with activity. Just be sure you're not pushing yourself too hard (see "Don't Get Too Much of a Good Thing," page 96). And remember: The very active person *must* eat well-balanced meals. Consult "Food for Fitness," page 91, and "Nutrition" for the specifics.

45 to 74 points: If last week was the norm for you, then you're certainly fitness-conscious! Either you're participating in regular aerobics or doing a lot of little things that add up. Within your total score, be sure you've included at least three aerobic activities during the course of the week (see #1 under "Evaluation"). If you've got that covered, the rest of your exercise is icing on the cake. If you don't, then you should see "Five-Step Aerobics," page 57, for the aerobic workout basics.

Under 45 points: Could it be you've forgotten some of last week's activities? It's not easy to remember every errand and chore. Starting this week, write down your activities as you go. If you increase your score, then that's great. If not, you'll benefit from the fitness advice that follows.

Joseph Cracchiola / FPG International

Disease Defense

It's clear that regular exercise helps lower your risk of heart disease and osteoporosis. Some studies even suggest that fit bodies fight off other illnesses, too. For example, a Harvard researcher found that women who played college sports had fewer incidences of certain kinds of cancer. Supposedly, exercise moves foods through the digestive system faster, shortening the body's contact period with cancerous food substances (see "Nutrition"). This and other news about exercise as a possible prevention of cancer isn't final; many other studies are still in the works. Yet research like this makes exercise look better all the time.

Good Looks

Have you ever noticed the difference in your complexion before and after a walk through the park? After the walk it looks fresh and alive. Exercise won't work miracles, but it will make subtle improvements in your skin, hair, and general appearance. Like good nutrition, the right dose of exercise helps your body system work smoothly, so it's likely to respond with healthy good looks.

Joe McNally/Wheeler Pictures

Just as good nutrition has a positive effect on complexion and hair, so too, does exercise. Physical activity revs up the blood circulation, which has a great effect on the entire body.

Working Off Extra Weight

Caroline gains a few pounds, and the first thing she does is cut back on high-sugar and high-fat foods. Not a bad idea, but Caroline would also be wise to exercise. In fact, Caroline could help her weight-loss plan by just eating a well-rounded diet and increasing her exercise.

Here's an explanation of how exercise works to burn energy. When you eat food, you are in effect eating energy. The amount of energy in food is measured in calories. Exercise burns, or uses, that energy. When the amount of calories consumed exceeds the amount of energy burned, you gain weight—one pound (.37 kilograms) for every 3,500 unused calories.

The equation is simple: Calories taken in equals calories burned plus calories stored. If you cut back your calorie intake, the body will rely on stored fat as energy. That's good, but without exercise you lose muscles, too. Exercise promotes the use of stored fat as the primary energy source. It not only burns excess calories and extra weight, but also builds up muscles. Muscle tissues need more calories than fat, so the muscular body can handle a higher calorie intake per day than the fat body.

What's more, exercise keeps working on your body—even after you stop exercising. Working out raises your metabolism (cell activity), so the body continues to use extra energy hours after you stop. Finally, here is a calorie-burning bonus: Exercise seems to suppress appetite. Who feels hungry after a few laps around the track?

Of course, regular exercise will cause these changes in your body even when you're *not* overweight, and that's good, too. Ideally, we all should be working toward this nutritionally sound, calorie-burning balance; the body works best this way. (Before you try any weight-loss plan, read "Good Reasons Not to Diet," Nutrition.) For those who do have extra weight to lose, exercise is a surefire cure. For those who don't, a fit body can help assure smooth sailing now and in the future!

Kaitilin O'Shea

STEP ON IT!

Running is probably the oldest sport known to men and women, yet every day people rediscover it as a rewarding form of exercise. Some like to take it a little slower and walk their way to fitness. If you move at a brisk pace, walking can provide an excellent workout. Use the chart below to help you determine how fast and how far you go when you're walking. Fit your walking workout in whenever you can—perhaps on your trip to and from school. Don't forget you need to sustain your speed for at least twenty minutes. Keeping track of the steps you take to get from class to class doesn't count. Try to speed up a bit or go a little further as you improve your fitness level.

Steps Per Minute	Minutes Per Mile	Miles Per Hour
70	30	2
90	24	2.5
105	20	3
120	17	3.5
140	15	4
160	13	4.5
175	12	5
190	11	5.5
210	10	6

Tiffany Cohen

You've heard it again and again: swimming is great exercise. Here are some of the reasons:

1) It provides an excellent aerobic workout. Your heart is actually larger when you are horizontal in the water than when you are vertical on land. This means it pumps ten to twenty percent more blood with each heart contraction.

2) It's great for toning muscles without the stress and strain of other jarring workouts such as jogging.

3) It increases flexibility because it elongates muscles while strengthening them.

4) All you need for swimming is a pool, a bathing suit, and sometimes a cap or goggles. It's usually inexpensive and convenient.

studies Tell All: Why Exercise?

○ In a recent study involving a group of schoolgirls, scientists found the overweight ones actually ate fewer calories than the slender ones. How could that be? The results indicated that the lean schoolgirls were two-thirds more active than the overweight girls.

○ A separate study compared swimmers, runners, and nonexercisers of the same age and height. The athletes ate 600 calories more than the others, yet the nonactive people weighed 20 to 30 percent more. This means that if the athletes weighed 100 pounds (37 kilograms), the others weighed 120 to 130 (45 to 47 kilograms).

○ Another case concerned girl swimmers at camp. Doctors observed that lean campers liked to race each other. The overweight girls, however, often stood around in the water, splashing and paddling.

Time and time again studies rule in favor of exercise. At your age you shouldn't be overly concerned with extra weight (see "The Body Trap," Nutrition). Nor do you want to overdo exercise (see "Don't Get Too Much of a Good Thing," page 96). Still, exercise is one of the best habits to develop. By enjoying it now while you're young and happy and healthy, you're more likely to stay that way!

Soccer is a tough, fast, exciting game, requiring great physical endurance. Once a game starts, it barely slows down, since the players move up and down the field almost continuously.

Joe McNally/Wheeler Pictures

Energy Pay Off

The right kind of diet can make all the difference in the way you feel (see "Energy And Performance," Nutrition). So can the right kind of exercise! When you treat your body to regular workouts, it learns to use and store energy better.

Exercise also chases away depression and tension (see the next section), major causes of fatigue. Finally, physical activity helps keep the body in good working order, so you sleep better. Exercise and a good night's rest may be all the insurance you need to ace that history test tomorrow.

Calorie-Burning Costs

Some 65 to 70 percent of the calories you use on a normal day are burned for vital body functions: heartbeat, breathing, cell replacement, and the like. Stress—like presenting a book report to your classmates and teacher—steps up your body's pace, making your heart beat faster, and consequently making your calorie consumption soar (see "Stress and Mental Health"). Tense situations, illness, menstruation, heat—they all accelerate your calorie-burning rate. But the biggest energy-eater of all is pure physical activity.

The following list shows the number of calories you burn per minute for various activities. The figures here are based on a 105 to 115-pound (39 to 43-kilogram) person. Calorie consumption increases with body weight. If you weigh less, you'll burn fewer calories per minute. If you weigh more, your energy consumption will be higher.

ACTIVITY	CALORIES BURNED PER MINUTE
Studying	1.7
Bedmaking	2.9
Horseback riding (walk)	3.0
Dancing (rock)	3.4
Lawn mowing (not riding)	3.5
Mopping floor	3.6
Baseball (outfield)	3.7
Walking (slow)	3.9
Gym class calisthenics	3.9
Swimming (casual)	4.0
Raking	4.1
Roller skating (casual)	4.1
Badminton (singles)	4.6
Water skiing	5.0
Gardening	5.1
Bicycling	5.4
Tennis (doubles)	5.6
Aerobic dancing	5.8
Stair climbing	5.9
Horseback riding (trot)	6.0
Basketball (half court)	7.3
Volleyball	7.8
Swimming (speed)	7.9
Snow shoveling	7.9
Roller skating (high speed)	8.4
Jogging	8.6
Running	8.9
Cross-country skiing	9.2

Joe McNally/Wheeler Pictures

Psychological Pluses

The next time you're mad, take it out on a punching bag. The next time you're depressed, cheer yourself up with a game of one-on-one basketball. True, physical activity won't solve all your problems, but it will make you feel better—better than eating or sleeping or worrying will. Dancing to a favorite tape or swimming around the pool can help you forget about your problems for a while, perhaps giving you a sense of control in life.

You may have heard adults talking about "unwinding" after a hard day's work. After a rough day at school, some physical activity helps you relieve stress, too. There's a very real physiological reason for this. When you experience a stressful event, the body tenses and immediately creates extra energy. Although the stressful event may be as minor as a typing test, the body reacts as if it's in danger and prepares to use this energy to run or fight.

This stress reaction is called "fight-or-flight," and it's normal and necessary for human survival (see "Stress"). However, this unused energy can build up and cause health problems. Exercise "spends" stress energy and helps the body return to a normal state. That's why stressed people feel so much better after exercise, and another reason why exercise is wonderful for you.

Physical activity also helps when we're troubled by anger, depression, fear, and other emotions related to stress. People with emotional disorders have been shown to improve with regular running and swimming programs. What's more, a Michigan researcher recently reported that exercisers seem to make friends more easily and have better personal relationships. While the explanations for these remarkable findings are a bit complicated, the lesson to be learned is simple: Exercise works wonders on both the body and the mind!

You can get exercise in many ways—it doesn't have to be in an aerobics class or at football practice. Playing one-on-one at a neighborhood basketball court or taking a bike ride around the block are other great activities.

Joe McNally/Wheeler Pictures

True or False?

Menstruating girls should avoid exercise.

False! In most cases, menstruation should not affect your workout. In fact, exercise can help relieve some menstrual discomforts. Compared to other females women athletes actually have fewer problems with cramps. Apparently, physical activity helps "loosen" the contractions in the uterus that cause cramps. Exercise also helps correct the hormonal imbalances that cause cramps.

That's not to say a day-long bike hike is the answer to ongoing menstrual discomfort. You'll have to judge what feels best during this uncomfortable time of the month, but don't pass up phys. ed. class on principle. Doctors assure us that exercise before, after, and even during menstruation is a better cure than painkillers and bed rest. Note: If you periods are extremely painful, consult a doctor. She may have some other answers for you (see "Human Sexuality").

What Is Metabolism?

A. The process that changes the food you eat and the air you breathe into activity is metabolism. Through this process, the heart pumps, fingernails grow, cuts heal, the head turns, and the legs move. Exercise speeds up this chemical change, so your body uses more nutrients and more oxygen in a shorter time.

Joseph Crachiola / FPG International

Fitness History

Is Dad a regular fitness machine? Or is a trip to the mailbox his idea of a workout? As a child, did you spend your recess playing hide-and-seek? Or did you prefer to read a book?

Your Fitness History won't tell you if you run a five-minute mile, but it might point out some old habits and attitudes you never noticed before. Consider for a few moments the kind of things you and your family like to do with your spare time.

Are you the sort of person who likes to go shopping or toss a football? What kind of chores do you enjoy—working in the flower garden or window washing? As a child, did you play Red Rover or climb trees, or did you and your brothers and sisters like to go horseback riding or play table tennis? Does your Mom work in the garden in her spare time and is your Dad good at golf or weight lifting? Think back to your favorite vacation. Was the main activity sightseeing? As a reward for a job well done, did you get tickets to a ball game or the ballet?

If you can answer yes to at least five of these questions, then for you and your family, exercise is a fairly big part of your life. However, you may not be working your heart hard enough, since most of the activities you chose are nonaerobic. Pay special attention to "Heart-Smart Aerobics," page 33 and "Five-Step Aerobics," page 57.

If your family's inclination is to take the high-energy road, then you're more likely to go cross-country skiing or jogging in your spare time. Chores you might do are cutting the grass with a push mower or heavy gardening. As a child your favorite game was running a race or pushing the merry-go-round, and with your brothers and sisters you went cross-country skiing.

If you're the sort of person who likes these sorts of aerobic activities, chances are you learned these habits from your Mom and Dad who might run laps around the track or climb mountains on the weekends. The typical reward in your family for a job well done might be a trip to basketball camp and your favorite vacation of all time was the one when you went skiing or hiking. All of these activities are excellent for the heart, but you should be sure that you're not overdoing the workouts. (See "Don't Get Too Much of a Good Thing" on page 96, plus the guidelines to a healthy exercise program in the next few pages.)

It could be that you and your family prefer eating and watching television to exercise. If the chores you do around the house consist only of unloading the dishwasher or washing and drying dishes, and your favorite childhood activities were playing with dolls or cars or listening to music, then give some thought to how inactive you are. Exercise should be an important part of your life, and you may not realize how little you're getting without taking this close look. You're probably the sort of person who needs to do more planning and thinking about fitness than more active people might.

As always, it's important to check with a doctor before you jump feet first into a rigorous exercise program (see "Exercise for the Maximum Benefits," page 55). Once you get the okay, you'll be ready to take on the healthy tips that follow.

Joe McNally/Wheeler Pictures

The family that plays together stays together. Sports and other acivity-oriented recreation let you share good times while boosting your health. (The exercise occurs after the ride when you carry the sled back up the hill!)

Fitness Is More Than Muscles

Granted, muscles are a big part of fitness. Without them, you couldn't lift a finger, let alone do more strenuous things like hitting a home run. But a healthy body isn't necessarily one with bulging biceps. In all, there are seven factors that determine physical fitness.

1. The most important element is *endurance,* the body's ability to stand up to stress for a long period. Skipping rope for ten seconds isn't difficult, but ten minutes is something else. Endurance is essential because the longer you exercise, the more you work and strengthen your heart and other muscles. While endurance workouts don't have to dominate *all* your physical activity, heart-smart exercise should be a priority (see "Heart-Smart Aerobics," page 33).

2. Muscular *strength* is also a must. You don't have to be able to lift the kitchen table with one hand in order to be strong, but a certain amount of strength is essential to good health. Strength and endurance work together in aerobic workouts.

3. The ability to bend, twist, and stretch the joints is *flexibility.* The more flexible your body is, the easier it is to move in and out of different positions without discomfort or in-

jury. Most sports require some flexibility. Wrestling and ballet, for example, require tremendous flexibility. When a dancer does a split, he or she has developed his or her flexibility.

4. *Equilibrium,* the ability to balance, is used every day just to climb stairs or walk down the street. But some athletes, like ice skaters and gymnasts, must develop this fitness factor in order to excel.

5. *Coordination* refers to the ability of the entire body to act and interact smoothly. One kind of coordination is being able to rub your stomach and pat your head at the same time. But coordination also enables you to see a Frisbee coming, run to catch up with it, reach for it, and throw it back. Coordination isn't a must for every form of exercise, but it plays a part. Some people seem to have natural coordination, but this fitness factor can be developed, too.

6. *Speed,* the measure of how fast body parts can move, is one indication of athletic ability, but it's not essential for every sport unless, of course, you're running the 100-meter dash.

7. Football players rely on *agility* when they react with quick, sure movements to dodge other players. If you're not agile when you play dodge ball in phys ed class, you're not going to be in the game very long.

WHAT DO YOU GET OUT OF YOUR FAVORITE PHYSICAL ACTIVITY?
Find out from the chart on the right which forms of exercise help develop which fitness factors.

Flexibility is the ability to bend, twist, and stretch the joints.
Coordination is the ability of all the parts of the body to interact smoothly.
Equilibrium is the ability to balance yourself.
Agility is the ability to move quickly with grace.
Speed is the measure of how fast the body moves.
Strength is the level at which your muscles are able to resist force.
Endurance is the body's ability to handle stress for an extended period of time.

	Flexibility	Coordination	Equilibrium	Agility	Speed	Strength	Endurance
Badminton	✓	✓		✓	✓		✓
Ballet	✓	✓	✓	✓	✓	✓	✓
Baseball		✓		✓	✓		
Basketball		✓	✓	✓	✓		✓
Bicycling					✓		✓
Bowling			✓				
Calisthenics	✓	✓	✓	✓			✓
Canoeing						✓	✓
Diving	✓	✓		✓			
Figure skating	✓	✓		✓	✓		
Fishing		✓					
Football				✓	✓		✓
Frisbee	✓	✓		✓			
Golf		✓					
Gymnastics	✓	✓	✓			✓	
Hiking							✓
Hockey		✓	✓	✓	✓		✓
Horseback riding			✓				
Jogging							✓
Judo	✓			✓	✓	✓	
Jumping rope		✓		✓			✓
Karate	✓	✓		✓	✓		✓
Pool		✓					
Racquetball	✓	✓		✓	✓		✓
Rowing						✓	✓
Skateboarding	✓	✓	✓	✓			
Skiing	✓	✓		✓			✓
Soccer	✓	✓		✓	✓		✓
Softball		✓			✓		
Swimming		✓				✓	✓
Table tennis		✓		✓	✓		✓
Tennis		✓		✓	✓		✓
Track and field					✓		✓
Volleyball	✓			✓	✓		✓
Waterskiing			✓				
Weight training						✓	
Wrestling	✓			✓	✓	✓	✓

What Do You Want to Improve?

The physical tests in "Measure Your Fitness Aptitude" (page 38) will show you what skills you can improve. But what fitness components are *you* interested in? Maybe increased flexibility would improve your cheerleading performance. Or some agility work would make you a better quarterback.

If you're interested in lowering your risk of heart disease because of your family history, want to ski (cross-country or downhill) without getting tired, strengthen your heart, be able to withstand stress as you get older, or sleep better at night, then you need to work on *endurance*, which you build with aerobics. This is a good choice. Aerobic exercise not only increases the strength of your heart, it also helps you handle stress, gives you more energy, and improves your sleep.

If you want to work on *strength* then you probably want to be stronger in gymnastics or be able to carry heavy books, groceries, or furniture with less effort. Choose strength-developing activities from the chart on page 40.

Equilibrium is the key to gracefulness. You want to work on this aspect of fitness if you're interested in horseback riding or dancing.

If you'd like to run faster than your brother, be quicker at volleyball, or beat the defense in football or basketball, then you need to think about improving your *speed*. *Agility* also figures into fast action in many sports, so it wouldn't hurt to work on that, too. It will improve your Wednesday afternoon volleyball and your dancing on Saturday night.

Everyone, no matter what his or her sport, should work on flexibility to reduce the risk of injury. A few stretches before working out will help prevent muscle strain as well as help you avoid stiffness as you get older. *Flexibility* exercises will loosen your joints and muscles for simple daily activities as well as during exercise.

A better sense of *coordination* will improve your pool playing, your performance in the marching band, or your batting score.

Think first about what you're interested in and then go from there to decide which fitness skills you should work on. Chances are you'll have to work on a combination of two or three, but it's a good idea to focus on the ones that are most important to you.

Bicycling is good exercise for many reasons. First, it's aerobic. Second, it puts very little stress on your joints, unlike high-impact aerobics or jogging. Still, bicycling does have its risk of injury. To minimize your chances of getting hurt, wear a helmet.

Heart-Smart Aerobics

Aerobics are exercises that demand a lot of oxygen, and significantly increase your heart rate. In order to benefit from aerobic exercise, you must:

1. exercise three to five times a week;
2. work hard enough to get the heart rate up (we'll give you the specifics later);
3. keep exercising for fifteen to thirty minutes without stopping.

This is called the Frequency, Intensity, and Time (FIT) rule. By exercising under the above conditions, your heart is getting the maximum benefits. You might say the aerobic workout is "designed" for heart health. Aerobics improve your endurance, flexibility, strength, and other fitness factors.

Usually you have to use the biggest muscles in your body—mostly in the arms and legs—to achieve these aerobic benefits. Of course, not all activities demand this kind of energy. That doesn't mean those exercises are not useful, it's just that they do different things for your body.

Nonaerobic exercise, which requires less oxygen and doesn't increase your heart rate as much, can develop your strength and agility. However, if you have time to fit only one kind of exercise into your schedule, it's probaby smart to concentrate on aerobics, which will develop your endurance and overall fitness. In fact, we suggest you develop an interest in two or three aerobic sports or activities that you can do for the rest of your life. Why more than one? This way, you're more likely to work on all seven fitness factors instead of just one or two. Plus, you'll find exercise a lot more exciting when it's varied.

In Part II of this book, we tell you how to check your heart rate and begin and end an aerobic workout. In the meantime, here are exercises generally considered to be aerobic:

- jogging
- swimming
- bicycling
- jumping rope
- tennis (singles)
- basketball
- running
- skating
- brisk walking
- cross-country skiing
- soccer

Joe McNally/Wheeler Pictures

One ballet movement is the arabesque, *in which the dancer stands on one leg, bends forward from the hip, and extends the other leg up and back. Most ballet movements require great physical strength.*

Joe McNally/Wheeler Pictures

Short-Work Nonaerobics

In aerobics you exercise at a steady rate. You're working hard, but you're able to supply your body with enough oxygen to fuel your body for at least twenty minutes.

You might be wondering about activities that don't satisfy the FIT rule, such as running the 100-meter dash. Is sprinting aerobic? While a 100-meter dash does accelerate your heartbeat (intensity) and can be performed three times a week (frequency), it isn't aerobic because you don't sprint for twenty minutes or more (time). Most of us can't sprint for twenty minutes or more; we can't take in enough oxygen to satisfy the rate at which we're exercising (the reason why you have to "catch your breath" after a fast, quick race). However, many of us can jog for twenty minutes and that's what separates aerobic running from nonaerobic running.

Of course, some highly trained athletes can sprint for twenty or more minutes, because they have advanced to a certain endurance level. These athletes are able to supply their bodies with enough oxygen to accommodate the high exercise rate. A nonathlete can also train his or her body to work at a faster aerobic rate. The first

time you jog for twenty minutes, you might find yourself gasping for breath. After a few weeks, however, you'll find that you're able to run faster and longer while breathing easily.

Remember, though, that while nonaerobic activities may not work your heart as well as aerobics, they do develop other fitness factors, such as speed or agility (see chart on pages 30–31). Something as simple as running for the bus is a nonaerobic activity, as are the exercises below:

○ baseball
○ bowling
○ football
○ kickball
○ tag

○ softball
○ ballet
○ gymnastics
○ tennis (doubles)
○ weight lifting

Nonaerobics aren't always performed in fast, short spurts, like a 100-meter dash or a run to third base. They also include sports or exercises that simply don't satisfy the FIT rule. Golf is a good example. This sport develops coordination, but participants won't accelerate their heart rate or keep moving at a fast pace for twenty minutes—unless they walk briskly for twenty minutes between each shot.

ow to Turn Nonaerobics into Aerobics (and Vice Versa)

The exercises we listed as aerobic or nonaerobic are usually considered to be just that. By paying attention to the FIT rule, however, you can change the "status" of the following:

A. Changing skating from an aerobic activity to a nonaerobic activity:

Skating is aerobic when it's performed at a constant, heart-accelerating pace for at least twenty minutes. Skating is nonaerobic when you skate for five minutes and stop, skate five minutes and stop again. Or, when you skate too fast for three minutes and you have to stop for a while to catch your breath.

B. Changing weight lifting from a nonaerobic activity to an aerobic activity:

Highly trained weight lifters can make their activity aerobic by first getting their heart rates up, then lifting quickly without pause. (Note: This is difficult to do and is only advised for adult experts.) You can achieve the same results with ballet, by dancing vigorously without stopping.

Lifting weights promotes extra strength. Sports doctors advise, however, that weight training is safest and most effective for young people after the age of puberty (age 12 for girls, 14 for boys) because the adult sex hormones that aid in body development are not present until then.

Roger Bester

WASHAEROBICS:

How to Get Fit While You're Doing the Dinner Dishes

Coming This Fall: The Adventures of Aerobic Man!

NEW! MISSY MUSCLE'S AEROBIC WEAR!

The Generic Aerobic

Aerobic Pizza:

One Bite and You're Bouncing With Energy!

Fashion, food, videos, and TV shows: Aerobics are consuming the country! But what do pizzas or hair-care products have to do with the FIT rule?

Not much. That's why you should be aware of the difference between an authentic aerobic workout and the generic use of the word. When a word or concept becomes popular, advertisers and marketing people use it to sell products. For example, you've probably seen the word "fiber" used on many food product packages. Because high-fiber foods have been linked with several healthy benefits, manufacturers are overusing this word—sometimes out of context—to sell their products. They know people are interested in fiber (or fitness or aerobics), and know the word will win attention (see "Nutrition").

You don't have to be skeptical every time you see the use of the word "aerobics." Exercise videotapes labeled as "aerobic" may or may not feature an aerobic workout. How can you tell? See if the workout satisfies the FIT rule. As for other "aerobicized" products, you decide whether or not you're interested. Just don't confuse the meaning of aerobics with its generic use.

True or False?

You have to work up a good sweat to get fit.

False! In most cases, aerobic exercise causes you to perspire—that's how the body cools itself off. But don't use sweat as an exercise gauge or fitness device. Less taxing activities, such as bowling or table tennis, may not cause you to perspire. That's normal, since these activities don't require hard work. On the other hand, overworking and sweating in a sauna in order to succeed at a sport (a common practice for wrestlers who try to lose weight so they can qualify for a certain competitive class) are lost causes. Excess perspiration does not cause weight loss. Instead, it depletes your body of something that's *essential* for health and exercise: water (see "Food for Fitness," page 91).

This isn't to say you should limit exercise to limit perspiration—sweating brought about by a good workout is perfectly normal and downright healthy—only that you shouldn't think you can "sweat off" extra weight and that you should drink plenty of water to replace perspiration. Six to eight glasses per day is the minimum; more is even better. Be sure to drink before and after exercise (see "Nutrition").

Measure Your Fitness Aptitude

There are many tests designed to measure your physical fitness. Here are two of them you should at least try. You won't be able to take these tests in your chair at the library, but you can copy some of them down to try at home. Get a friend to help you. (Note: the tests have some similar exercises.)

Test I *

1. *Curl-ups (abdominal strength/endurance)*
Have someone hold your feet and time the number of curl-ups you can do in one minute. Lie on your back with knees flexed at 90 degrees. Your heels should be no more than 12 inches (30 centimeters) from the buttocks; your back should be flat on the floor. Cross your arms close to your chest and keep them this way throughout the exercise. Now, raise the trunk by curling up to touch elbows to thighs, then lowering the back to the floor. (Your upper back should actually touch the floor.) Don't "bounce" off the floor and don't remove your fingers from your shoulders. How many can you do in a minute? Be careful about your back; never jerk yourself up, but come up slowly.

2. *Pull-ups (arm and shoulder strength/ endurance)*
You'll need a horizontal bar that's high enough for you to hang from with arms fully extended, feet off the floor. Using an over-hand grasp, raise your body until the chin is over the bar but not touching it. Then lower the body back to the hanging position. Don't swing your body or kick or bend your legs, and strive for a smooth—not jerky—movement. How many can you do? (No time limit.)

3. *V-Sit Reach (flexibility of lower back and posterior thighs)*
With chalk or adhesive tape, draw a 2-foot (60-centimeter) line on the floor. Now, mark another line intersecting the first line, or baseline, in the middle (a yardstick will help keep it straight). Mark the intersection "0." On the second line, place 1-inch (2.5-

centimeter) and .5-inch (1.2-centimeter) marks.

Remove your shoes and sit on the floor. The measuring line should cut between your legs. Your heels should be 8 to 12 inches (20 to 30 centimeters) apart and behind the baseline.

Clasp your thumbs so that the hands are together, palms down, and put them on the floor between your legs. At this point, a friend should hold your legs flat. Flexing your feet and keeping them perpendicular to the floor, slowly reach forward along the measuring line as far as you can. Keep your fingers on the floor and don't bounce. How far can you reach? Practice three times, then record the distance on the fourth try. If you reach 1.5 inches (3.8 centimeters) *beyond* the baseline, then your score is + 1.5. If you reach behind the baseline 2 inches, your score is –2. Get it?

4. *1-Mile (1.6-kilometer) Run/Walk (cardiovascular and respiratory endurance)*
Have someone time you as you run and walk 1 mile. Your gym teacher can help you measure the distance. The idea is to finish as quickly as possible, but it's okay if you need to intersperse running and walking.

5. *Shuttle Run (leg strength/endurance/power/ agility)*
You'll need two blocks of wood about 2 inches (5 centimeters) wide by 2 inches high by 4 inches (10 centimeters) long. Chalkboard erasers will do too. If possible, do this test on a volleyball court. Otherwise, you'll need to draw two parallel lines about 30 feet (9 meters) apart. Put the wood or erasers behind one of the lines.

Begin by standing behind the *other* line. While a friend times you, move as fast as you can to the wood, pick one block up, run back to your starting line, and place the block *behind* the line. Then, run back to the other block, pick it up, and run across the starting line with it.

The less time it takes you to do this, the better your score. You're not allowed to throw the block across the line.

How did you do on these five parts? They're from the Presidential Physical Fitness Award program, and in order to pass, you have to do at least as well as eighty-five percent of other students your age.

Note: If you would like to compete for the Presidential Physical Fitness Award, write: The President's Council on Physical Fitness and Sports, Washington, D.C. 20001.

*From "Fitting In," a publication of the American Alliance for Health, Physical Education, Recreation and Dance.

Nancy Coplon

President's Physical Fitness Award Passing Scores

AGE	CURL-UPS (number per minute)	PULL-UPS	V-SIT REACH (inches)	1-MILE (1.6-KILOMETER) RUN (minutes: seconds)	SHUTTLE RUN (seconds)
Boys					
12	50	7	+4.0	7:11	9.8
13	53	7	+3.5	6:50	9.5
14	56	10	+4.5	6:26	9.1
15	57	11	+5.0	6:20	9.0
16	56	11	+6.0	6:08	8.7
Girls					
12	45	2	+7.0	8:23	10.4
13	46	2	+7.0	8:13	10.2
14	47	2	+8.0	7:59	10.1
15	48	2	+8.0	8:08	10.0
16	45	1	+9.0	8:23	10.1

The pull-up and variations of the pull-up are not only a required calisthenic exercise in the President's Council test: the U.S. Marines and U.S. Army use it, too.

Tobey Sanford/Wheeler Pictures

Stretches aren't what they used to be. For example, experts now tell us that a stretch like this one could be harmful, since it strains the hamstrings in the back of the leg and the back muscles. This girl should slightly bend her knees and avoid forcing herself to the point where she feels pain.

Bud Freund/Wheeler Pictures

Test II**

1. *Back Muscle Strength and Flexibility*
   Place a pillow on the floor, then lie down with your stomach on it. Have a friend place one hand on your ankles and another on the small of your back. Now lift your trunk off the floor. You pass if you can hold it for 10 seconds.
2. *Lower Back Muscles*
   Stay on your stomach with the pillow in place. Have your friend steady your back with both hands. Now raise your legs off the ground—knees straight—and hold. If you can hold for 10 seconds, you pass.
3. *Back Muscles and Hamstrings*
   Stand up straight, feet together. Roll down as far as you can. If you can touch the floor, you pass.
4. *Abdominal Muscles*

Clasp your hands behind your head and lie flat with your knees flexed. While a friend holds your ankles, try to roll up to a sitting position. Did you pass?

5. *Hip Flexors and Abdominals*
   Lie flat with your legs extended. Have a friend hold your ankles. Roll up to a sitting position. You pass if you can do this once.
6. *Hip Flexor Strength*
   Lie on your back with legs extended. Keep your knees straight and lift your feet 10 inches (25 centimeters) off the floor. Can you hold it for 10 seconds? If so, you pass!

**From Kraus-Weber tests for flexibility and strength, *American Health*, May 1987.

Why the Difference Between Girls and Boys?

Levels of fitness are sometimes different for girls and boys. Reason: Because of their different physical makeup, female and male bodies have different athletic strengths. For example, male shoulders are wider, so their upper bodies are often stronger. Females, on the other hand, tend to be more flexible. As boys mature, they get stronger, taller, and heavier than girls, so the overall physical performance of the average male exceeds the average female for most sports.

The average woman is not only built on a smaller scale, her circulatory and respiratory system also operate less efficiently and she has a higher percentage of body fat to muscle as compared to a man. These differences shouldn't prevent any woman or girl from living up to her athletic potential. While it's true that the average man's athletic ability exceeds that of the average female, a champion female tennis player can beat an average male tennis player (see "Human Sexuality").

Tag football is only one of many ways you can incorporate exercise into your life and have fun, too.

James Kirby

43

What Can I Do To Improve My Fitness Level?

In Part I you read about *why* exercise is important. In Part II you'll discover how fitness relates to you and how to create a plan that you can follow—not necessarily one to get you into the Olympics, but one that will help you introduce exercise into your life. An exercise schedule shouldn't be as cut-and-dried as a class schedule; variety lends fun and interest to any activity. With these things in mind you'll set up your own plan, and get all the basics to help you through a healthy, safe, rewarding, and exciting workout. It's a challenge you'll love!

Geoffrey Clifford/Wheeler Pictures

In a track and field meet, runners race around an oval track (above). In the field in the middle of the track, athletes compete in throwing and jumping events.

Make Your Own Exercise Plan

Now that you've evaluated the kinds of things you like to do, you have some idea of what exercise will best meet your fitness needs and preferences. If you picked cross-country skiing, that's great, but how are you going to manage that when you live in Miami? Unfortunately, location, time, and even money constraints can limit our fitness possibilities. But there are plenty of fitness options, and one is bound to be just right for you.

Finding the Possibilities

On your own paper, draw a chart like the one below. Write in all the sports and activities available to you for each category. (We've given you a few examples.) You may have to consult your phys ed teacher or make a few phone calls in order to have a complete record.

ORGANIZED SCHOOL SPORTS	COMMUNITY LEAGUES	OUTSIDE CLASSES	CLUBS	ON YOUR OWN
Track	Bowling	YWCA	Health spas	Home videos
Intramurals	Church team softball	Recreation center	School ski club	Biking
Soccer	Business-sponsored teams	College dance	Golf	Running
etc.	etc.	etc.	etc.	etc.

s Your School on the Ball?

Physical fitness is so important to health that most governments are very interested in how much their young people exercise. In the United States, the President's Council on Physical Fitness and Sports has some guidelines that all schools should strive to satisfy. Where does your school's physical education program stand? Answer "yes" or "no" to the following questions:

1. Do you have at least one class a day in which a teacher or coach leads you in vigorous physical activity?
2. Is there a part of your gym class devoted to activities like running, fast-paced calisthenics, agility drills, and weight training?
3. Does your school program offer instruction or some sort of participation in lifetime sports, such as tennis, swimming, skiing, and jogging?
4. Does your school give any tests that reveal specific physical problems? For example, some students may be unusually weak, inflexible, overweight, or uncoordinated and need special help in these areas.
5. Are there any special programs for people with physical disabilities?
6. Are all the students in your school tested for physical fitness aptitude at least twice a year?

If you answered "no" to some of these questions (1, 2, and especially 3), you should take an interest in upgrading your school's PE program. Get a parent or teacher to help you and take these steps:

1. First, find out what your local school code says about physical education. What requirements are specified in state laws or regulations? This is your ammunition, but even if these regulations are limited, it's worth pushing for a better fitness program.
2. Talk to your school's PE instructor first. Ask questions and see if he or she can help.
3. If the instructor can't make the necessary changes, then have your parent or teacher see the principal. Perhaps the PE instructor will be able to make recommendations for changes in your exercise program.
4. It might also be necessary to win the support of your school's parent-teacher association, since big changes in the school's financial priorities and scheduling may be necessary.
5. Is the problem not your school's policy, but the whole school district's? Then take the issue to the local board of education.

Considering the Possibilities

What activities interest you on the chart you just made? List them on another chart, including at least two aerobic exercises. Then fill in the requested information as shown in the chart below.

As you can see, some sports are a little harder to participate in, but they're probably well worth the effort. Some of the activities you might have chosen can't be done every day—and that's fine. Fitness should be fun—not a ritual—so it's important to include a variety of activities in your weekly plan. The next chart will help you plot a clearer picture.

ACTIVITY	INSTRUCTION/ SKILL	TIME	SEASON	MONEY
Cross-country skiing	Lessons as a child; won't need	Saturdays and Sundays	Winter (only when there's snow)	Ski and boot rental
Roller skating	None needed	Evenings and weekends	Any	Skate rental; admission to rink
School basketball team	Provided but must make tryouts	Practice every day 3–5; games Tues. and Sat. at 7	Oct.–Feb.	None
etc.	etc.	etc.	etc.	etc.

BODY STRESS SIGNALS

Just as it is your responsibility to work a fitness program into your life, you must listen when your body tells you during a workout that something is wrong. Here's a chart that will help you recognize when your body is saying "Stop! I've had enough!" and will help you decide what to do.

Stress Signal	Action
Abnormal heart action • irregular pulse • fluttering, jumping, or palpitations in the chest or throat • sudden burst of rapid heartbeats • sudden drop in pulse rate	Stop! Walk slowly until your heart rate returns to normal. Don't exercise again until you've seen your doctor.
Pain or pressure in the center of your chest or in your arm or throat	Stop! Walk slowly until your heart rate returns to normal. Don't exercise again until you've seen your doctor.
Dizziness Lightheadedness Sudden incoordination Confusion Cold sweat Glassy stare Pallor Blueness or fainting	Stop! Lie down and elevate your feet or put your head down between your legs until the symptom passes. Don't exercise again until you've seen your doctor.
Continued high heart rate 5 to 10 minutes after you've stopped exercising	Slow down the next time you work out and monitor your heart rate to keep it at the lower end of your target zone. If you still have an excessively high recovery heart rate, see your doctor.
Nausea	Lighten the intensity of your workout and be sure to warm up and cool down completely.
Gasping for air after workout	Lower the intensity of your workout; continue lowering it until you can hum a tune to yourself while you work out.
Side stitch, side ache (diaphragm spasm)	Slow down and breathe deeply into the spasm until it relaxes.
Joint or muscle pain	Stop and adjust your body alignment.

Planning the Possibilities

Draw another chart on a piece of paper like the one below. Write in your ideal fitness plan (we show you how). Remember, this plan isn't set in stone. Maybe you'll find more interesting activities during the course of the year and tire of others. You might get more and more involved in wrestling and make that a priority, or you might decide a health club membership isn't for you. The idea is to exercise regularly. This chart will help you make a long-term plan.

MONTH	MAIN ACTIVITY	FILL-IN WORKOUTS	OCCASIONAL THRILLS
January	Aerobics classes	Home videos Shoveling snow	Skiing
February			
March		Walking	
April	Biking	Gardening	
May	Biking Tennis		
June		Swimming	Windsurfing
July	etc.	etc.	etc.
August			
September			
October			
November			
December			

Your Weekly Workout

Now draw an ideal week of workouts. Look at the yearly chart you just drew—what sports did you write down for this month? Your weekly workout might look like this:

MONDAY	TUESDAY	WEDNESDAY	THURSDAY	FRIDAY	SATURDAY	SUNDAY
	Aerobics class		Aerobics class	Dance		Downhill skiing

Be sure to include one exercise satisfying the aerobic FIT rule on page 33:

1. *Frequency:* For the best results, you must work out three to five times a week.
2. *Intensity:* Your workout has to be hard enough to get your heart rate up (see page 59).
3. *Time:* While your heart rate is in target range, the workout must last at least twenty minutes.

Once the FIT rule is taken care of, you can fill in other nonaerobic activities, leaving yourself time for rest (see "Don't Get Too Much of a Good Thing," page 96). In the week we planned above, the aerobics classes and dance satisfy the FIT rule while downhill skiing is a nonaerobic activity— but nevertheless an important one!

You're on your way! Turn the page for how-to's.

Skiing was developed as a form of transportation by people who lived in heavy-snowfall regions. But today, it's a popular recreational and competitive sport all over the world.

Michael Melford/Wheeler Pictures

Joe McNally/Wheeler Pictures

he Fun Factor

Forget "no pain, no gain." Fun is a fundamental part of exercise; without it, most of us wouldn't be as interested in fitness. In fact, a 1981 study showed that Canadian men cited "fun and excitement" as the second best reason for exercising; "feeling better" was first. The women put "feeling better" first, "weight control" second, and "fun and excitement" third.

With news like this, it's clear that fun is important, and many doctors say that by choosing an activity we enjoy we're more likely to make exercise a regular part of our lives. People who don't like their exercise, on the other hand, often stop doing it.

So while you're making out your personal exercise plans on these pages, make fun activities a priority. Analyze the activities you've enjoyed in the past (swimming at camp? softball?). Try new sports, and approach familiar sports in different ways (play tennis with a new partner, shoot basketball on a different court). Don't pressure yourself to exercise more than you need to; sometimes an activity overload destroys the fun factor. And if you haven't already, try the test on the next page ("Are You Having Fun?") for more insight.

In volleyball, players hit a ball back and forth across a high net, often jumping high to put more force on a ball's return. It's simple enough for general exercise, yet requires enough skill to be played as a competitive sport.

Are You Having Fun?

We can talk about heart strength and a good night's sleep all day, but fun is a big part of exercise, too. Granted, mopping the floor probably won't end up on anybody's "Favorite Sports" list. Yet, there are lots of forms of exercise that provide plenty of fun and are a great way of avoiding the monotony of working out.

Listed are suggestions for ways you can incorporate your other interests (such as music, the outdoors, etc.) into an exercise plan. By following these tips, exercise won't be a bore, but something that you can really have fun with.

○ If *music* inspires you to get moving then try aerobics classes or home videos that incorporate music into their workouts. At home ride an exercise bike or dance while you play the stereo. If you own a portable cassette player or radio with headphones, walk or run to your favorite band.

○ Maybe you prefer *team efforts* to exercising alone. If so, join a sports team or gather your friends for Saturday afternoon volleyball.

○ If you like to work at your *own pace* without too much pressure or regimen, you probably like to *work alone* rather than on a team. Try biking, jumping rope, jogging, walking, swimming, or skating—or try exercising to a workout video. These are just a few of the exercises you can do by yourself.

○ For many people it's easier to follow a *structured plan* rather than discipline themselves. If you participate in aerobics class, you'll have instructors to guide and encourage you. Home videos also offer a pre-planned workout. And, of course, if you join a team, you'll have coaches to monitor your activity.

○ You might prefer *simple tasks* to challenging ones. Try jumping rope, trampolining, dancing, running, biking, or walking. These are all activities that don't demand high levels of skill in order to be enjoyable and good for you.

○ If you're the sort of person who likes to work at something until you *master the skills* you'll probably enjoy skating, skiing, racquet sports, and most games involving a ball; these activities should keep you athletically challenged. (Maybe you should look into organized sports. People who are interested in mastering a skill or excelling may have what it takes to be an Olympic star or an All-State player!)

○ Maybe *competition* is what motivates you. If so, join a school sports team or, if you prefer more casual competition, consider tennis, handball, or running with a friend.

○ If you love *scenery, fresh air, and the great outdoors*, then instead of exercising indoors with a stationary bike, take it outside. Walking, baseball, water sports, and winter sports are other fine outdoor activities.

HOW DOES EXERCISE PAY YOU BACK?

When you're first starting to exercise, you'll have to keep reminding yourself why you're doing it. This chart shows you the payoffs, so look at it whenever your willpower is on the wane. Pretty soon you'll see the results for yourself.

Appearance Payoffs
• Firmed and toned muscles
• Proper body weight maintained
• A healthier, more attractive appearance
• Walking taller and standing straighter

Physical Fitness Payoffs
• Increased energy, stamina, and vitality
• Increased muscle strength and endurance
• Improved coordination and reflexes

Health Payoffs
• Body fat content reduced
• Circulation stimulated, heart strengthened
• Need less sleep, sleep more soundly
• Increased resistance to illness and disease
• Tension and stress relieved
• Decreased risk of heart attack
• Longer life

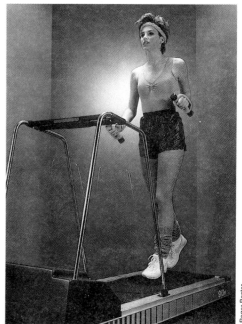

Roger Bester

Psychological and Performance Payoffs
• Ability to work harder without becoming fatigued
• Skills sharpened for sports and recreation
• Increased self-discipline
• Increased mental alertness and concentration
• Increased self-esteem and confidence
• Sense of pride about being physically fit
• More relaxed approach to life
• Have more control over your life

Exercise for the Maximum Benefits

Do you feel like you're ready to start exercising right away? Are you ready to tear up the track? Dance 'til you drop? That's terrific, but there are unhealthy ways to do it and smart ways to do it. Before you begin any exercise program, double-check the following:

○ Your Personal Health: most people your age don't need a doctor's approval, but you do if you have any heart problems, breathing trouble, dizzy spells, diabetes, or other special health conditions. Also, don't exercise until you've completely overcome any illness—influenza, colds, mononucleosis, etc.—since overexertion might keep you under the weather longer.

○ Proper dress: You don't have to have the latest in leotards or the newest thing in shoes, but you should dress appropriately when you exercise. Be sure your gear is right for your activity; some designer outfits may be unhealthy for indoor workouts because they promote overheating. Indoors or out, choose loose-fitting clothes that allow you to move freely. Your shoes should be sturdy and cushioned; ask your coach or phys ed teacher for more details about what shoe is best for your sport (see also, "Shoe Review," page 80, and "Nice Weather We're Having," page 79).

○ Water and Nutrition: A lack of either will not only result in poor performance, the added strain of exercise on your already-taxed body could make you sick. Remember: So-called sports drinks are not as healthy as the equivalent amount of water (see "Food for Fitness," page 91).

Idea

Why not make a "Workout Contract" with a friend? Get it in writing that you'll take an aerobic class (or run, skate, or swim) together three times a week. This way you'll have someone to share your goals and fun with. Plus you'll give each other support on those "lazy days." After all who doesn't need some encouragement now and then?

○ Time: Avoid strenuous exercise during extremely hot, humid weather and within two hours after you've eaten.

Take It Easy!

You may have been playing baseball since you were big enough to lift a bat, but that doesn't mean you'll be able to jump feet first into a full-blown aerobic workout. In baseball you developed your speed, coordination, and agility, among other fitness factors. But it's doubtful you worked hard enough to satisfy the FIT rule (unless you ran around the bases for twenty minutes, three times a week!).

The same is true of any nonaerobic sport or activity. If you participate regularly in any form of exercise, you probably have some well-developed fitness skills (flexibility for ballet, equilibrium for horseback riding, for example). Yet you'll have to take gradual steps to develop your endurance, the keystone to aerobics. Pacing yourself carefully assures that: (1) You won't injure yourself by overexerting underdeveloped muscles; (2) Your heart will have a period in which to adjust to the new demands your body is making. Strengthening your heart doesn't happen overnight.

The guidelines in "Five-Step Aerobics" will help you start an exercise program that avoids injury and slowly strengthens your heart. Stretch and warm up before your workout. Then work hard enough to work your muscles, breathe deeply, and perspire. After the workout, cool down and stretch again.

Don't push yourself too hard. Aim for a workout every other day. One extra-long, extra-hard workout per week defeats the whole purpose of conditioning the heart and won't give you the same results. It takes a few weeks of regular aerobic workouts before your heart gets the total benefits (see "Heart-Smart Aerobics," page 33).

Also, don't try to make vast improvements from workout to workout. Some people add an extra lap every time they swim or run around the track. By overdoing it too early in the game, you might hurt yourself. And you might not have as much fun as you would by taking it more slowly. Gradual changes in your routine will reap as many benefits, if not more (see "Set Realistic Goals," page 82). Besides, you're not training for the New York City Marathon—you're doing your health a favor and improving your lifestyle. To do that, you have to sweat a little and try a lot, but it's worth the effort.

Ask yourself: Do I prefer working out indoors with other people? Then you might enjoy an aerobics class. However, if you like to be outdoors and on your own, jogging might be more your speed.

Steve Smith/Wheeler Pictures

Five-Step Aerobics

For the healthiest aerobic workout (no matter what kind it is), follow these steps:

1. Stretch at least 5 minutes.
   Beginning a workout without stretching first is like waking up with an ice-cold shower. Tight muscles aren't prepared for vigorous exercise, and they react by straining or pulling. Stretching lengthens muscles, filling them with blood to make them pliable. The result is a safer, more rewarding workout. It's not only smart to begin every aerobic workout with stretches, but nonaerobic activities as well (see "Smart Stretching," pages 60–74).
2. Warm up, 5–10 minutes.
   After stretching, you'll ease yourself into your aerobic workout. This gradually raises your body temperature and heart rate, bringing more blood and oxygen to the muscles and preparing them for more vigorous exercise. Even the fittest among us have to warm up before a workout; it helps performance and lowers the risk of muscle or joint injury (see "Warm-up Wisdom," page 75).
3. Aerobic workout, at least 15–20 minutes.

The actual workout satisfies the FIT rule, whether it's cross-country skiing or swimming (see "Heart-Smart Aerobics," page 33, for ideas). The key to aerobics is to get your heart into the target range (see page 59) and to keep it there by moving constantly until the workout is over. For example, if you're playing singles tennis, you should jog lightly in place or walk and swing your racquet while your partner chases a ball.

4. Cool down, 5–10 minutes.
   Just as you don't want to plunge into a workout, you don't want to stop suddenly when your heart is still in the target range. If you do, your muscles may feel stiff and sore. Without first cooling down, you could experience cramping, dizziness—even fainting. Essentially, the cool-down is the same thing as the warm-up. Following the directions in "Warm-up Wisdom" on page 75, you can bring your heart rate down gradually, thus reducing the risk of injury after the workout.
5. Stretch, at least 5 minutes.
   Repeated exercising tends to shorten muscles. If you don't limber up your muscles with post-workout stretches, those muscles could go into spasms. Stretching also *feels* good—and after a fine workout, you deserve to feel good.

ow to Take Your Pulse

Your pulse is the key to determining if your workout is getting your heart rate into the target range. To take it, you'll need a watch that shows seconds. Check your heartbeat every 5 minutes, but don't stop moving for more than 30 seconds while you do this or your heart rate will slow down. You can take your pulse in several different places, but the carotid artery, found in the neck, is the easiest to find.

To find your pulse:

1. Put the tips of your index and middle fingers of one hand at the point where your jawbone comes up under one earlobe.
2. Slip your fingertips down the side groove of your neck about 1 inch (2.5 centimeters).
3. Press in gently. You should be able to feel your heart beating.
4. Using your watch, count the beats for exactly 10 seconds.
5. To calculate your heart rate per minute, multiply that number by 6.

The chart below tells you what your target rate should be for 10 seconds or 1 minute. If you get your heart within this range, then you're getting the full aerobic benefits: a stronger heart, more lung power, a psychological lift, and more. If you don't hit your target range at first, don't get discouraged; it sometimes takes a while to reach it and regular exercise will help. However, if your heart rate always falls below the target range when you exercise, then you need to work harder or find a more taxing sport. Maybe you could move around the basketball court more, dribbling and passing with more energy. Or maybe you need to move faster and swing your arms when you walk.

It's also possible to work up a heart rate *beyond* the target range. This means you're working too hard and risking injury. If this happens, slow your run down to a brisk walk or push your bike up a big hill instead of pedaling so hard.

TARGET HEART RANGE FOR AGE:	TEN-SECOND COUNT	ONE-MINUTE COUNT
11–13	21–30	145–175
14–16	20–28	144–173

Kayaking requires pulling on oars to move a boat. Many people enjoy kayaking on lakes and rivers for outdoor exercise.

Smart Stretching

A stretch is not a painful, bouncing movement. In fact, avoid all bouncing. This only shortens and tears the muscles, the exact opposite of what stretching is supposed to do. Stretching is a gradual relaxation of the muscle, which lengthens and warms it up. Each movement should be performed for 15 to 30 seconds, while you continue to breathe fully at a normal rate, relaxing a little further into the stretch with each exhalation. Remember: Do not bounce! You can tailor your stretches to your aerobic activity or do a few general ones. Here are a few examples.

General

Upper Body Rolls: Stand up straight. Place your hands on your hips, with your feet placed shoulder-width apart. Slowly lean forward and roll your upper body around in a circle. Don't let your hips move, and keep your back and shoulders straight. Roll to the left, then to the right. Repeat 5 times in each direction.

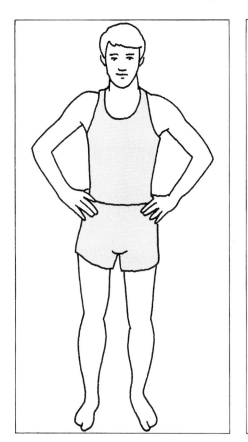 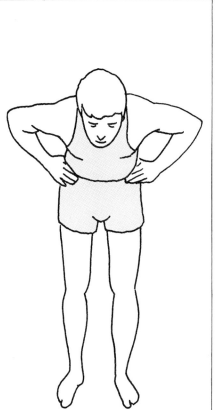 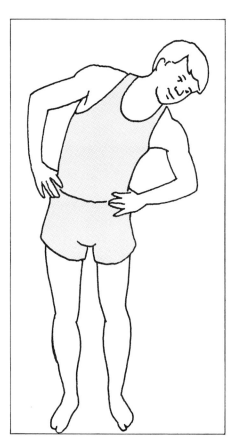

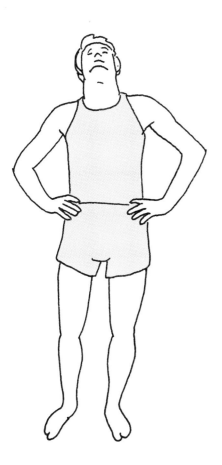 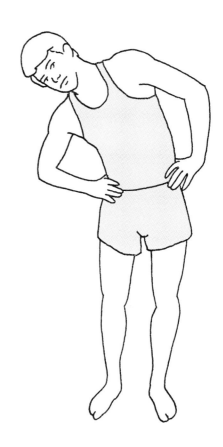

After any exercise, it's important to stretch out the muscles you've worked. This helps you maintain flexibility and lessens your chance of injury.

Bud Freund/Wheeler Pictures

Arm Stretches: Stand up straight. Hold your arms above your head, with your palms facing toward the ceiling. Pretend that you're trying to touch the ceiling with your palms and slowly push your arms behind you. Don't bend at the waist. Hold for 15 seconds.

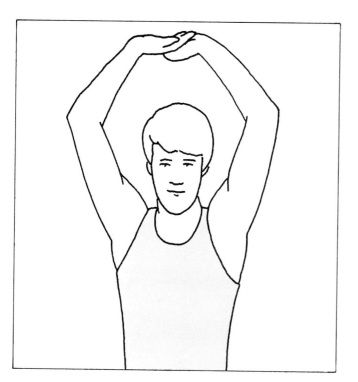

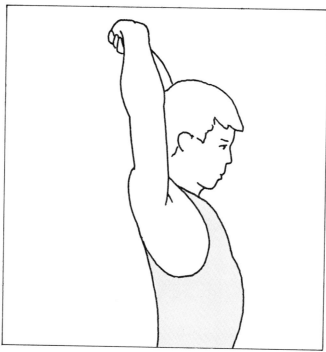

Waist Twists: Stand with your legs bent slightly and your hands on your shoulders. Twist your upper body from side to side, keeping your lower body still. Continue for 10 full twists.

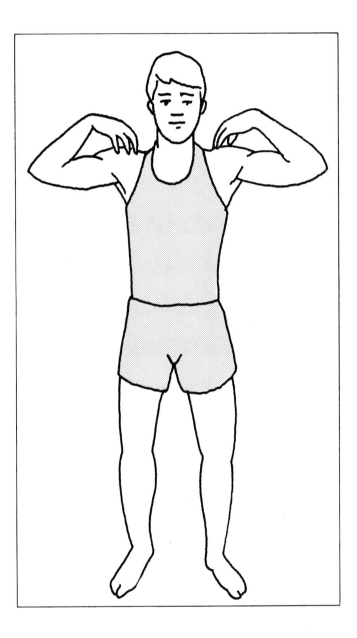

Hamstring Stretches: Sit on the ground, placing your legs in front of you at a comfortable distance apart. Slowly lean forward, keeping your back straight. Put your hands in front of you for balance and hold for 20 seconds. Now put your legs together and bend forward, reaching for your toes. Don't bounce, and keep your knees and feet pointing to the ceiling. Hold for 20 seconds.

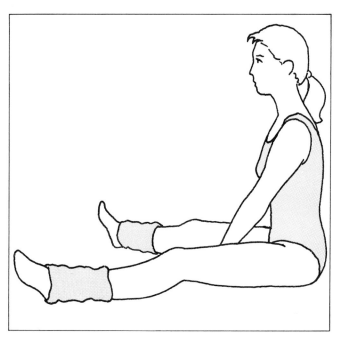

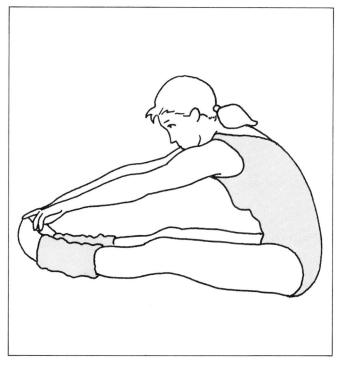

Courtesy of Rodale Press

Running

Split Stretches: Stand with knees straight, then slowly spread your feet apart as far as you can. Bend over and press your palms against the floor between your feet. Hold for 10 seconds. Repeat 5 times.

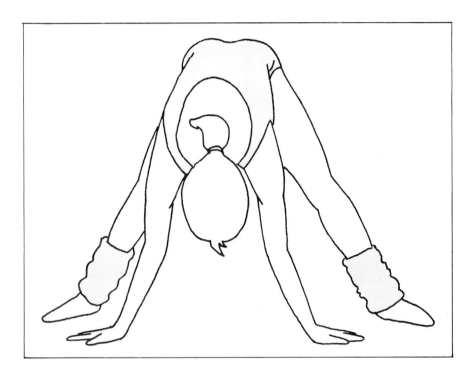

Lower Back Stretches: Lie on your back and bend your knees. Raise one leg, grasp the knee with both hands, and bring it to your chin. Hold for 10 counts, then release. Do the same with the other leg. Repeat the exercise 10 times for each leg.

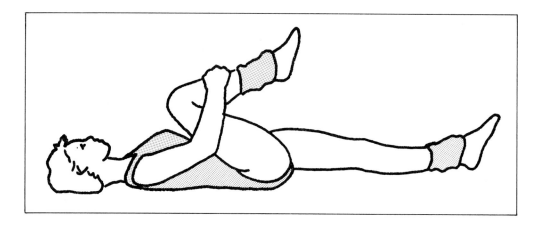

Wall Push-ups: Stand an arm's length away from a wall and rest your palms flat on it. Keep your body straight, your feet parallel, and your heels on the floor. Now bend your elbows and move the upper part of your body toward the wall. Hold for 10 seconds. Return to starting position and repeat 5 times.

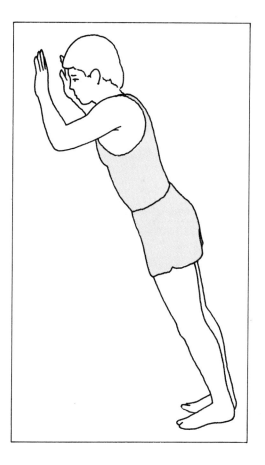

Injuries cause many joggers to quit. Though every physical activity involves some risk, your chances of getting hurt are less if you make pre-run stretching a rule. Don't forget to stretch after the workout, also.

Nancy Coplon

Tennis

Neck Rotations: Stand or sit. Rotate your head 5 times to the left, then 5 times to the right.

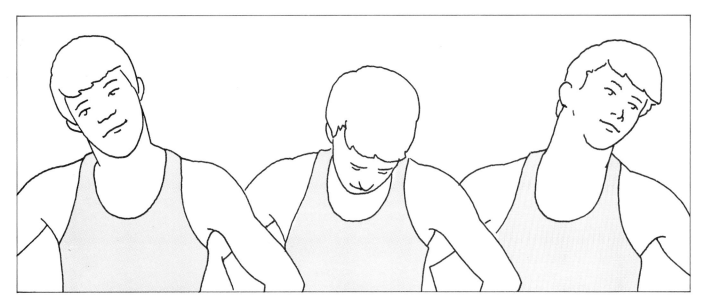

Joe McNally/Wheeler Pictures

Arm Circles: Stand up straight and slowly rotate and stretch your arms back for 10 seconds—as if you were doing the backstroke. Stop and row in the other direction for 10 seconds.

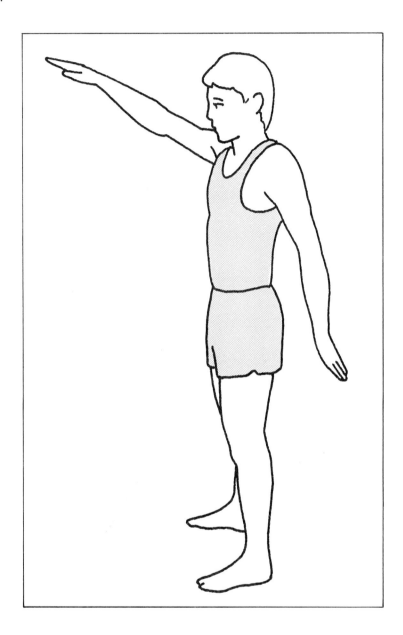

In the 1400s, the French started a game that was similar to the tennis we play today. The first tennis tournament was played at Wimbledon in 1871.

Reach-up Stretches: Stand up straight and stretch and reach toward the ceiling with your right arm. Switch to your left arm. Do this 10 times.

When a player leaps high to make an overhead smash (below), a lot of power is placed behind the ball, so that the opposing player has a more difficult time returning it.

Joe McNally/Wheeler Pictures

Sprinter Stretches: Get down into a sprinter's position with your fingers touching the ground on both sides of one foot, bending at the knee so it's at a right angle with the body, and extending the other leg straight behind you. Stretch your Achilles tendons and calf muscles by pointing your back heel and lowering your hips. Repeat with the other leg. Do 5 sets.

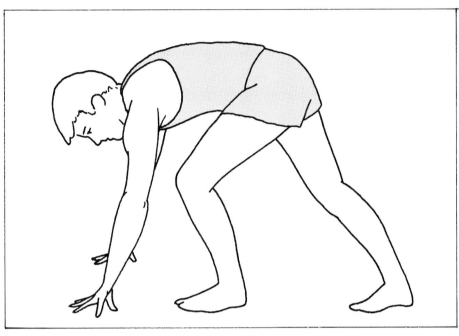

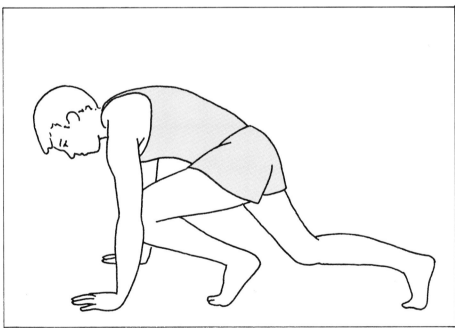

Skating

Twist and Stretch: Stand with your legs shoulder-width apart. Keep your knees straight but not locked. Bend forward from the hips and reach for your left foot with the right hand. Stand up straight. Reach for your right foot with the left hand. Repeat 20 times.

Ankle Stretches: Sit with your legs straight in front of you and your heels touching the floor. (1) Rotate your ankles for 15 seconds in each direction. (2) Point your toes out for 5 seconds. (3) Pull your feet toward you for 5 seconds. Repeat this 3-step stretch 5 times.

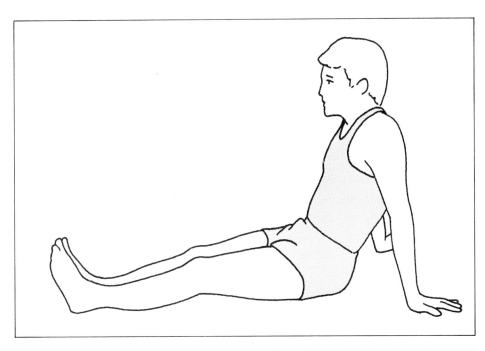

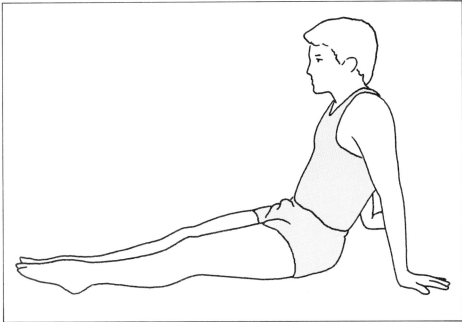

Leg Lifts: Place one leg on a ledge or wall to make a right angle with your torso. Keeping your knees straight (but not locked), lean toward your raised foot. Hold for 10 seconds. Put your foot down and repeat with the other leg. Do this 5 times per leg.

Note: While each of these stretches have special benefits for particular sports, they're all good warm-ups for most any activity. Mix and match them all you want, as long as you take it slowly and don't *ever* stretch to the point of pain. Move slowly and hold each stretch 5 to 10 seconds. Discomfort is okay, but when it starts to really hurt, it's time to release some of the tension. Pain is a warning signal that you should take seriously.

The most important things to remember about stretching are: Go slow and easy, and don't bounce. If you are stretching correctly, it should not hurt.

*W*arm-up Wisdom

An exercise warm-up is like a rehearsal—after stretching, you go through the motions of your workout, taking it slowly. This chart will give you an idea of how to warm up for your sport.

TO WARM UP FOR:	DO THIS:
Running	Walk briskly
Tennis	Hit some balls back and forth
Swimming	Swim a few slow laps
Walking	Walk slowly
Biking	Pedal slowly, then coast, then pedal

Ken Levinson

Breathe!

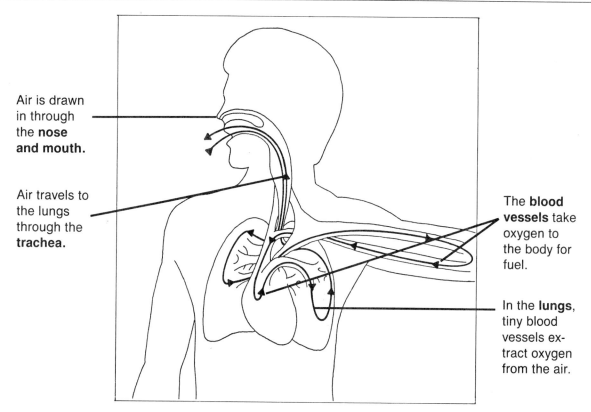

Air is drawn in through the **nose and mouth.**

Air travels to the lungs through the **trachea.**

The **blood vessels** take oxygen to the body for fuel.

In the **lungs**, tiny blood vessels extract oxygen from the air.

Sometimes it's easy to get caught up in a sport, concentrating so hard that you forget to breathe properly. Yet oxygen helps fuel our movements, so it's tremendously important to breathe deeply while we work out.

What happens when you don't breathe deeply and regularly? When you breathe in, the lungs fill with oxygen, taking up all the space in the rib cage, pressing on the blood vessels in the chest. If you hold it in while you exercise, pressure is increased. This can reduce blood flow to the brain and make you feel faint. And naturally, that hinders your performance.

What's the best way to breathe? Some theories say to breathe in through the nose, breathe out through the mouth. Others emphasize inhaling and exhaling patterns coordinated with muscle-tightening or foot-falls. No evidence proves these special breathing patterns improve performance, but they might help athletes take their minds off a hard workout as well as ensure proper breathing habits. The important thing is to concentrate on breathing in deeply and breathing out fully, in a regular rhythm. Slow down when you find yourself gasping for air. If it helps you to breathe in a particular pattern or with your mouth, that's fine. Talking to someone else or singing to yourself as you exercise will help you be sure to breathe regularly. It doesn't matter how you do it, as long as you just keep regular breathing in mind.

Nonaerobic Workouts

Should you apply the five-step aerobic plan to other exercises? Because your heart isn't operating within the target range with nonaerobic exercises, it isn't necessary to gradually increase your heart rate with warm-ups and cool-downs. But it *is* important to stretch your muscles before and after your workout whatever the sport (see "Smart Stretching," pages 60–74). In fact, for some nonaerobic exercises, like ballet, track, and football, stretching to improve flexibility and prevent muscle strain is a *must*. Many sports participants like to warm up amply for a better performance. Basketball players, for example, practice lay-ups, dribbling, and foul shots, while volleyball players warm up by jumping at the net and serving the ball.

Joe McNally/Wheeler Pictures

Even if you don't exercise vigorously each and every day, your body and mind can benefit from 10-15 minutes of stretching. This relaxes tight muscles and reduces stress on supporting ligaments and tendons.

Everyday Fitness Opportunities

As we've pointed out several times, exercise is more than gymnastics and jogging. You can also reap benefits from day-to-day activities such as housework, yardwork, errands, and the like.

Some of these activities can be strenuous enough to become aerobic activities. If that's what you're going after, be sure to follow the "Five-Step Aerobics" plan on page 57. Other everyday fitness opportunities help develop fitness factors (strength, equilibrium, coordination, and so on) and burn calories (see "Calorie-Burning Costs," page 24).

Here are some opportunities to get in shape you might not want to miss. Mom and Dad will no doubt be happy to help you think of other ideas!

Shoveling snow*
Climbing stairs*

Sweeping the porch*
Walking to the store*
Raking the lawn*
Washing the windows (or the car)
Hand-mowing the lawn*
Mopping the floor*
Vacuuming the carpet
Scrubbing the bathtub (or the floors)
Walking the dog*
Hoeing the garden*
Carrying groceries (or the trash out)
Pushing a baby carriage (or a child in a swing)*
Shaking out rugs
Painting the kitchen
Weeding the garden
Clipping the hedges
Working on a farm*

*Activity could be aerobic; check the FIT rule.

ice Weather We're Having

The temperature outside has a lot to do with your workout. Just as you have to change your dress for the changing weather, you may also have to change your exercise schedule.

Handling Heat: It's best to limit outdoor sports when the weather is extremely hot and humid (above 80 degrees Fahrenheit or 27 degrees Celsius and/or 75 percent humidity)—if not by avoiding it completely, then by slowing down. Choose loose-fitting, lightweight clothes that are white or light-colored. Cotton is a good choice because it absorbs perspiration. Wear a hat and sunscreen to protect your skin from the sun's damaging rays.

While it's always important to drink plenty of water, it's especially important for hot-weather exercise. Drink water before, during, and after your workout. Otherwise you could overheat and suffer from heat cramps, stress, exhaustion, or even heat stroke. If you experience any of these symptoms—muscle spasms, excessive thirst, fatigue, pale skin, blurred vision, or dizziness—or a marked increase or decrease in perspiration—*stop immediately!* Move to a cool place and drink plenty of water. See a doctor if the symptoms don't disappear.

Coping With the Cold: Don't bundle up as you normally would for a winter day, because exercise will automatically raise your body temperature. Instead, wear one less layer (for example, leave off the heavy coat and wear a light jacket instead). By dressing in layers instead of one or two heavy pieces, you can take off layers as you warm up, then put them back on as you cool down.

Don't wear waterproof material, since it tends to trap heat and prevent perspiration from evaporating, which is how your body cools itself. Always wear a hat and cover as much of your body as possible to keep precious body heat from escaping.

Some serious symptoms that indicate overexposure to cold weather are blanching or numbness of toes, fingers, ears, chin, or nose; a "waxy" skin appearance; severe shivering; lack of coordination; and inability to speak. These are signs of frostnip, frostbite, or hypothermia. At the first sign of frostnip—blanching or numbness—go inside! Blow on the area. Hold the affected part against your body or place firm, steady pressure on it (do not rub the area as you may damage the skin) with a warm hand. Or immerse the frostnipped area in lukewarm (not hot) water. You'll know it's okay when the skin turns red and starts to tingle. If not, see a doctor immediately.

Frostbite and hypothermia are much more serious. If you or a friend experiences more than blanching or numbness, cover the victim with warm blankets and call the rescue squad. The best antidote, though, is prevention—if it's cold enough for frostbite or hypothermia to be a possibility, it's best to bring your workout inside.

Shoe Review

All marketing hype aside, athletic shoes really are important to healthy exercise. Because your feet are taking the brunt of your workout, you want to give them support, comfort, and protection. Your coach, phys ed teacher, or even a clerk at the local sports shop can help you choose the right shoe for your sport. In the meantime, here are the basics.

Tony Cenicola

eneral Tips:

Be sure there is adequate cushioning under the ball of the foot. The insole should be firm, but soft enough to absorb the impact of your foot on the ground. The heel cup should be solid but not too snug. Make sure the heel is firm but well-padded and that your foot doesn't move from side to side when you put your weight on it. The tongue and upper sole should be well padded and should stay in place as you move. The outside of the sole should be durable, yet lightweight. Can you bend the shoe at the bottom, where the ball of the foot hits? If so, you know it's flexible enough. The area beneath the arch of the shoe should be rigid and lie flush with the ground.

Walking:

Look for sturdiness and comfort, as well as ankle and arch support, and curved soles that seem to guide your foot through the walking motion.

Aerobics:

Lots of cushioning and support to keep your foot in place and prevent injuries.

Tennis:

Reinforced toes; extra padding at the ball of the foot; sturdy, stable sides (for the continuous side-to-side motions); cushioned, spacious toe box.

Bicycling:

This shoe should be flexible and breathe enough to allow comfortable walking, yet stiff enough to keep your foot on the pedal while you ride.

Running:

Soft, flexible, and lightweight; slightly elevated, reinforced heels, and high-impact soles.

A word about socks: These days, even the socks on the market are specialized. Generally, however, you should choose nylon or cotton blends (Orlon/nylon, nylon/ Lycra, or cotton/Spandex) that absorb moisture so it can evaporate quickly. On cold days, you might appreciate the heat-trapping comfort of Thermax socks, made of a lightweight polyester.

Socks shouldn't be overly snug, but not too loose and bulky either. A poor fit could promote blisters. For the best comfort and performance, get your sports shoes fitted while you're wearing your socks. Many varieties are available with extra padding or cushioning to accommodate your sport.

All runners need to pace themselves; otherwise, they run out of steam too early. This is equally true for a single run or a series of runs. Runners who try to increase their distances too quickly are more likely to get hurt and less likely to have fun.

Monitor Your Workouts

Now that you know the basics, now that you can judge what activities best suit and fit your needs and how to begin and end in healthy fashion, there are a few things that will help you start and maintain your exercise program.

Set Realistic Goals

Don't feel you must work up to Olympic standards or ready yourself for a college athletic scholarship. In fact, unrealistic goals might discourage you from continuing your fitness program. Instead of setting out to be an Olympic athlete on the first day:

○ Challenge yourself to regularly follow an exercise plan. If you drop out a month after you begin, you haven't accomplished much. For most people, a four-time-a-week aerobic workout is something to be proud of. That's a realistic goal, but one that requires discipline, too.

○ Introduce yourself to new sports. Once you meet your FIT rule on a regular basis, you'll feel more confident and interested in other exercises. Set a goal to try all kinds of different sports—even if you don't master them all, you'll increase your fitness level *and* fun factor.

○ Gradually increase the amount of exercise you do each week. Just to keep things interesting, follow a schedule that changes from week to week. While it's true that it will take several weeks to increase your jogging time from ten to twenty minutes, make the progression from week one to week four a more interesting one by monitoring your runs. Ideally, you'll work out three times per week, with one day separating each exercise day. The most important rule to remember is that you're not in this to break

any records. Just take it easy and have some fun. Your plan for a jogging program might look something like this:

Week 1: Stretch, 5 minutes
Jog slowly (warm up), 5 minutes
Jog briskly at target heart rate, 5 minutes
Jog slowly (cool down), 5 minutes
Stretch, 5 minutes
Week 2: Stretch, 5 minutes
Jog slowly, 5 minutes
Jog briskly, 7 minutes
Jog slowly, 5 minutes
Stretch, 5 minutes
Week 3: Stretch, 5 minutes
Jog slowly, 5 minutes
Jog briskly, 9 minutes
Jog slowly, 5 minutes
Stretch, 5 minutes
Week 4: Stretch, 5 minutes
Jog slowly, 5 minutes
Jog briskly, 11 minutes
Jog slowly, 5 minutes
Stretch, 5 minutes

○ Continue each week in the same manner, increasing your target heart rate workout by two minutes per week. By Week 12, you'll be jogging briskly for thirty minutes—a fine goal and a good workout. By Week 13, you'll be in such good shape, your heart may not reach the target heart range so you may want to intensify the activity by carrying light weights.

○ Once you reach this point, you don't necessarily have to continue to increase your workout, but you do have to keep up the good work. Otherwise, your body will slip back out of shape—in less time than it took you to get in shape.

Nancy Coplon

reat Expectations?

Do you exercise because

1. You want a body like those in the fashion advertisements?
2. Exercise enables you to eat all the desserts you want?
3. Someone (like a coach or parent) pushes you?

If you answered yes to any of these questions, you might be in for disappointment or health problems.

1. First of all, it could be impossible for you to have a body like the top fashion models. You're born with a particular body type, and though exercise *will* tone and slim it, all the workouts and diets in the world won't change the basic shape (see "Nutrition").

What's more, an ultra-slim figure may not be healthy for you, especially if you have to overexercise and overdiet to achieve it. At any age, but especially now when your body is still growing and maturing, it's best not to overexert yourself physically or deplete yourself of nutrients (see "Nutrition").

2. Since the calorie-burning benefits of fitness were first praised, some people think they can have their cake and eat it, too. The theory is that they can overload on unhealthy, fattening foods, and then "work it off" with vigorous exercise.

The calorie-burning benefits of exercise are clear. Dieters are wise to rely on exercise to help them meet their goals, as are normal-weight people. And a heavy workout schedule may very well burn those extra calories (see "Working Off Extra Weight," page 20). However, there are two major problems with this view of exercise and nutrition:

(A) Fattening foods like desserts contain much more than calories. They're also high in fat and cholesterol, food substances linked to cancer and heart disease, among other health problems. While you can work off those extra calories, you can't get rid of fat and cholesterol as easily. (Physical activity does push blood through your veins harder to help unclog cholesterol and may aid the speedy passing of cancerous food products out of the body, but you can't expect it to completely erase the effects of a diet heavy in cholesterol and fat.) What's more, a person depending on desserts or other nutrient-low foods is probably neglecting the important nutritious foods (see "Nutrition").

(B) Because high-fat and high-sugar foods are also high in calories, a great deal of exercise may be needed to overcome the effects of steady consumption of these foods. And because overexercising is just as unhealthy as not exercising at all, ultimately, it's best to cut down on sweet and fatty foods, eat a well-balanced diet and follow a monitored exercise plan to lose weight.

3. It's nice to have support, but sometimes coaches or parents get carried away. If you're working out to please someone else, you may feel pressured. Perhaps you're not having as much fun as you could if you were doing something *you* enjoyed. First, decide what *you* want to do. If your goal is to become a figure-skating champion, you may appreciate guidance from a well-meaning adult. But if it's Dad's dream—not yours—for you to win the state's long jump title, it might be time for you and Dad to talk. Tell him how you feel: You like to participate in field events, but you don't feel you have to be number one. Or you get queasy whenever you *think* about the long jump. Whatever. The most important thing is to choose activities you enjoy; otherwise, you won't want to exercise (see "Stress and Mental Health").

Nancy Coplon

Get involved! Unlike some sports, running requires little strategy. The goal is to cross the finish line first, or just to have fun.

Michael Melford/Wheeler Pictures

Snacks are okay, as long as the choices are healthy. While this man has a large appetite, he's smart to snack on fruits.

What Can *You Expect from Exercise?*

After your first workout, you'll feel good. Your muscles may be a little sore, but most of us even feel good about *that;* it's a reminder that you have the get-up-and-go to do something healthy for yourself. You'll probably feel more cheerful, relaxed, and clear-headed afterwards. Some people experience an energy high right after a workout; they're ready to shower, dress, and go to school or head for the ball game. Others may feel a little tired after the first few workouts, but in general, they feel more energetic.

After a few weeks of regular exercise, your body will be firmer and more flexible. When you're not working out, your pulse will be slower, a healthy sign. You might even notice subtle changes in your appearance; clearer, fresher skin; shinier hair; a better shape. But don't take our word for it, try it and see!

Joe McNally/Wheeler Pictures

Roger Bester

Before you begin weight lifting, get guidance from a knowledgable instructor, such as your physical education teacher. Remember: Lighter weights and more repetitions (number of times you lift a weight) develop muscle tone. Heavier weights and fewer repetitions add bulk.

Plot your progress

Dieters are often encouraged to write down everything they eat in a day. This helps them see how fast calories add up, where they went wrong and where they went right, and how to improve or change their diets to fit their needs.

The same can be said about a workout journal. It will be interesting to compare your diary with the plan you drew from page 16. Did you stick to it? Have you found an exercise you enjoyed more than you originally thought?

By writing down your actual workouts (everything from climbing seven flights of stairs to aerobic dance class), you can take pride in your accomplishments. You'll be able to look back and see you've only had two aerobic workouts this week so you can add a third before Sunday. You'll see any patterns leading to an exercise downfall. For example, you might notice that Friday night's late-late movie always makes you sleep past Saturday morning's church league softball practice. Or workouts on Tuesday, Wednesday, Thursday, and Friday exhaust you, so you don't feel like working out again until Tuesday. Insight like this helps you to reschedule for the best benefits.

To keep track of your progress you can use any calendar or notebook system. Record anything you think might be exercise (see page 78 if you need help). Your weekly calendar might look like this:

Monday:	Marching band practice, 1 hour
	Walked home from school,
	30 minutes
Tuesday:	Marching band practice, 1 hour
Wednesday:	Jogging (aerobic), 25 minutes
Thursday:	Marching band practice, 1 hour
	Carried groceries home from store,
	20 minutes
Friday:	Gym class, 40 minutes
	Marching band show at ball game,
	20 minutes
Saturday:	Jogging (aerobic), 25 minutes
Sunday:	Jogging (aerobic), 25 minutes

A complex carbohydrate, pasta is a true "get-up-and-go" food. Every year before the New York Marathon, the New York Road Runners' Club sponsors a huge pasta dinner. Participants in the next morning's race gather to stoke their energy supply before the rigorous exercise begins.

Food for Fitness

Pauline was Holston Junior High's star long-distance runner on the track team. Every race she didn't win, she ran a close second. So when the All-Conference meet came around, Coach Jordan and the other team members were counting on her.

What happened? Pauline didn't even place. She was tired. And while her loss could have been caused by a number of physical or psychological factors, the most probable reason was her diet for the day. Pauline didn't eat breakfast, and at lunchtime, she chose two white rolls and a soda from the cafeteria line.

Pauline might not have felt hungry or thirsty, but her body was. All of us need nutritious diets, and exercisers, who burn more energy, are especially dependent on good foods.

For starters, Pauline would have done herself a big favor by drinking plenty of water before the meet. Even on days when there is no track practice or meet, Pauline needs at least six to eight glasses of water. Exercise increases her need, since perspiration causes the body to lose water. It doesn't matter that she didn't feel a need to drink; we feel thirsty long after the body starts to need water. On track meet days and every day, Pauline should drink up before she feels thirsty.

What about those "sports" drinks you may have seen advertised? They're really not necessary or even your best choice. It's cheaper and healthier to rely on water. Drinks with caffeine (tea, colas) or sugar (sodas, punches) aren't good substitutes for water, either.

As for Pauline's meal plan for the day, she couldn't have hurt her chances for a fine performance more—unless she hadn't eaten anything. Breakfast was the first big mistake. The first meal of the day is the most important one, since it makes up for your sleeping hours and is the basis of your day's fuel (see "Nutrition"). A food high in protein (low-fat yogurt, skim milk), complex carbohydrates (whole-wheat toast, whole-grain cereal), and fruit (orange juice, banana) would have improved Pauline's schoolwork as well as her afternoon race.

At lunchtime, an athlete like Pauline should have concentrated on complex carbohydrates; these are foods that have that "stick-to-the-ribs" quality. They contain substances called glucose, known to provide energy to muscle tissue, the nervous system, and brain in steady, even amounts. Pauline might have chosen whole-wheat rolls, beans, pasta, vegetables, or fruit instead of the white rolls. Some protein (turkey, chicken, ice milk, low-fat cottage cheese) would have completed her meal. But Pauline and other exercisers would be wise not to believe that coaches' myth about eating steaks before competition. High-protein diets do more harm than good. While it's true some protein is necessary to *maintain* muscles, meat and other protein foods don't build muscles; exercises do. High-protein meals not only boost your fat intake, doctors believe they might even slow down your muscles.

In the future, Pauline would be smart to eat a well-rounded diet high in complex carbohydrates all the time. It might not help her win all her races, but it will help her do her best. To find out more, see "Nutrition."

Warning!

Don't exercise for an hour or two after you eat. While your body is digesting food, more blood is needed in the digestive tract. Exercise interrupts digestion by stealing that blood for the muscles, which could cause stomach pains.

The same holds true if you eat immediately *after* exercise—the blood you need for digestion might not be so quick to leave the muscles. The result again: stomach pains.

Motivate and Reward Yourself

Even the most dedicated among us have those oh-I-don't-want-to-work out days. If you're truly sick or if you're convinced that exercise would do more harm than good, you're probably wise to forgo it. But on days when you're suffering from nothing but the Lazy Blues, exercise might be the high-energy kick you need. It works wonders for the attitude, too (see "Pyschological Pluses," page 26). Chances are, once you manage to get started, you'll be glad you did.

It also helps to pat yourself on the back every now and then. Exercise is remarkable in that it gives you a great feeling of accomplishment. Be proud of a job well done! Reward yourself with a new book, a movie, clothes—even new sports equipment.

Now for some get-up-and-go strategies:

○ Wear snappy exercise clothes. A color-splashed leotard or brand-new sweatsuit may be all the inspiration you need.
○ Get a friend to join in. Wouldn't running be more fun with Jeremy? If Sara joined your exercise class, you both might get a boost.
○ Try something new. Switch to swimming instead of biking. Walk a new route. Play some music while you use your rowing machine.
○ Put off something you really want to do. Tell yourself you can go to the record store *after* you take a walk.
○ Plan something fun for after the workout. If you and Cindy have a late afternoon tennis game, then how about a movie afterwards? You'll both be inspired to work hard.
○ Read about exercise's health benefits on pages 14–16 and find out why more and more people are exercising every day: lower cholesterol; less risk of heart disease and cancer; weight control; a happier attitude; and a better-looking body to name a few.
○ Tell yourself how good you'll feel. Remember your last workout? That feeling of accomplishment? Go for it again!

The most important thing to drink before, during, and after your workout is water. But water only replenishes the fluids you lose in perspiring. Fruits or fruit juices boost your energy level both before and after exercise.

Rodale Press

xcuses, Excuses!

Don't be guilty of using any of these excuses:

"Exercise is boring."
It doesn't have to be! Just add some fun and variety to your workout (see "The Fun Factor," page 52).

"I'll get hurt."
Okay, so maybe you are more likely to sprain an ankle on a basketball court than you are on the sofa. Still, stretches and warmups will lower your injury risk considerably and so will moderation—no overdoing it, please. This way, the exercise's healthy benefits far outweigh the injury risk, and by strengthening the body through exercise you'll actually make it less susceptible to injury.

"It's embarrassing to run in my neighborhood."
You know better than that. There's no reason for you to be ashamed of getting into shape; it shows how health-conscious you are and that you like yourself. Besides— haven't you heard—fitness is in style. But if public exercise bothers you, choose another sport you can do in private. Or get up early in the morning and run before the neighborhood wakes up.

"Aerobics are too complicated."
Not if you follow the easy "Five-Step Aerobics" plan. The first time or two out, you may have to double-check our directions. Soon, though, taking your pulse and stretching will be second nature. In fact, the challenge of working up to your target range makes aerobics all the more interesting.

"I don't have time."
How much time do you spend watching television during a week? Sunbathing? Sitting on the school steps? Doing nothing? Surely you can find time to work in the aerobic minimum: three to four 20-minute exercise sessions per week. True, some of us are busier than others, but fitness is a worthwhile investment in your health. Take the time. If it helps, think of exercise as a social activity. Get your friends to join you in working out, and you'll probably discover yourself looking forward to it!

"I'm too tired to exercise."
Experiment. If you're exhausted after school, perhaps you'll feel better after rest and dinner (allow two hours for digestion), or before school. If early-bird workouts do *not* appeal to you, try afternoons or school gym classes. The point, of course, is to find your high-energy points. And remember: Exercise has an energizing quality. Once you get moving, you'll probably forget about being tired.

Aerobics get your heart into shape and burn calories, while calisthenic exercises, like these leg lifts, help tone muscles.

Roger Bester

Joe McNally/Wheeler Pictures

Perspiration is your body's cooling mechanism—the reason why you sweat in hot weather and whenever you exercise.

Don't Get Too Much of a Good Thing

Exercise is wonderful in moderate amounts. But some people get carried away with fitness. Their workouts are too long and too frequent. When that happens, health risks go up and health boons go down. Here's how:

1. While exercise is a great way of strengthening the body and thus lowering the risk of injury, overdoing it increases the potential for strained joints or muscles. Compulsive exercisers may ignore pain in these areas, but pain is a sign of injury. Without rest and recovery, the damage could eventually become serious or permanent.

2. *Some* exercise strengthens bones; too much can actually increase the risk of osteoporosis, a weak-bone disease (see "Nutrition").

3. Strenuous exercise can also interrupt a female's menstrual periods (amenorrhea) by burning off stored body fat essential to the production of hormones that help regulate menstruation (see "Human Sexuality").

4. Mentally, exercise overkill jeopardizes the fun factor. When fitness becomes a grind, it's not as enjoyable. People who go overboard may eventually lose interest in working out.

How much exercise is too much? Let your body be the judge; people perform best at different fitness levels. Generally, about one hour of vigorous exercise on any one day and a total of five hours per week maximizes the good-health bonuses. Another general rule: In some cases every-other-day workouts may actually be better than daily exercise. When you exercise hard, a day off allows your body to rest and heal the tiny muscle tears that often occur during a workout.

If you feel up to it and your exercise choice isn't extremely strenuous, daily activity is fine, too. In fact, many experts recommend that you exercise every day. Not that you want to cross-country ski for four hours each day; that's too much. But a walk or bicycle ride is easy enough to handle on a daily basis. By incorporating a variety of activities into your weekly routine, injury risks are smaller. On Monday you can take on the sweat-intensive aerobic class; Tuesday, a stroll through the park; Wednesday, hard-core aerobics again; Thursday, a bike ride. And so on.

Of course, if you injure yourself or get sick, you'll want to stop exercising until you're better. See a doctor if you stop menstruating or if pain persists. "Sports Injuries" on page 98 offers more advice.

he Jim Fixx Story

Jim Fixx was a world-famous runner who died of a heart attack while he was jogging. Some people use his story as an excuse to avoid exercise. What can we learn from this incident?

It's been argued that Fixx overexercised. That may be true, especially considering his health condition: advanced heart disease, an enlarged heart, and three past heart attacks. Maybe Fixx didn't need to work as hard as he did.

Yet, doctors say Fixx's exercise lessened his risk factors (before working out, he was fat, a smoker, and had a family history of heart disease) and he probably lived longer than he would have otherwise.

The lesson: Exercise is to be done in moderation and with common sense. Excessive exercise is as foolhardy as none at all. It doesn't necessarily cure all health problems. Other factors, such as your environment, family history, and personal habits also affect your health. Still, the evidence of exercise's healthy effects is too favorable to ignore. If you are in a high-risk group (say, your parents had heart disease, you're overweight, and you eat a high-fat diet) you may want to consult with a doctor before you undertake a long-term exercise plan, but you'll probably lower your risks considerably by staying active.

Sports Injuries

Exercise should not be painful. In a few cases, minor discomfort can be overlooked. In others, prompt attention is needed.

Blister: A "hole" worn in the inner layers of skin by friction; it collects pus.
Possible causes: Improperly fitting shoes; new activity.
Treatment: Apply rubbing alcohol and bandage if blister isn't broken. If blister is broken, wash with soap and water, trim top, apply alcohol.

Side Stitch: Pain felt in upper abdomen on either side.
Possible cause: Insufficient oxygen due to incorrect breathing.
Treatment: Continue to exercise until it disappears. Or stop, bend over at the waist, raise the knee of the painful side and press on the area with fingertips. Take a few deep breaths.

Shin Splint: Dull ache in lower shins.
Possible causes: Running and jumping on hard surfaces over a period of time; lack of warm-up stretching; sudden stops; shoes without support.
Treatment: Massage the painful area with ice for ten minutes. Ask a coach to watch you run to see if you're doing something wrong. Stretch and warm up before exercising. See a doctor if pain persists.

Charley Horse: Calf muscle cramp.
Cause: Hard blow to the front of the thigh, or walking or running on hard surfaces without proper arch support.
Treatment: Ice or cold pack on injured area; raising the thigh; rest. Contact doctor if you're in a great deal of pain.

Pulled Muscle or Strain: Sudden, deep pain in one area, usually felt when stretching or exerting yourself, doesn't involve the joint but may be felt below or above one.
Possible cause: Lack of pre-workout stretching, overstretching, bouncing, or overuse of muscle.
Treatment: Rest, ice, compression, and elevation. See a doctor if pain persists.

Sore Muscles: Discomfort occurs twelve hours after workout and becomes more severe the next day.
Possible cause: Sudden change in amount or type of exercise (common for beginning exercisers).
Treatment: Cool down after exercise.

Sprain: Pain, swelling, and discomfort around joint or ligament; discoloration.
Causes: A blow, twist, stretch, or stress on the ligament or joint between two bones.
Treatment: Wrap the sprained area; apply ice; elevate; rest. Have doctor check for fractures.

For treatment of a sprained ankle, follow R.I.C.E. instructions: Get Rest, apply Ice and Compression, and Elevate the problem area.

Surefire Steps to Injury Prevention

1. Use moderation. The key to any successful fitness plan is easing into it. You can bet that Martina Navratilova didn't become a champion in a year or two, and likewise, you shouldn't expect to get in shape over the course of a week. Follow the conditioning advice on page 82 (''Set Realistic Goals'') and take it easy.
2. Follow the five-step aerobic plan. Always, *always,* stretch and warm up before your workout, then follow it with a cool-down session and more stretching.
3. Try a variety of activities. Different exercises call for different muscle groups. Also, by alternating more strenuous workouts with less taxing ones, you'll give your body a rest. This allows the microscopic muscle tears that occur in every workout to heal.
4. Don't ignore pain. If you continue to exercise on an injured foot, a minor problem could turn into a serious one. Give your body a rest (see ''Don't Get Too Much of a Good Thing,'' page 96). Pay attention to any ache or pain that doesn't go away.
5. Check your fitness gear. Your shoes should provide adequate support (see ''Shoe Review,'' page 80). Clothing should be loose, yet appropriate for the season (see ''Nice Weather We're Having,'' page 79). If you're using other equipment—racquets, weights, bicycles—have them examined by a sports expert, such as a coach, phys ed teacher, or someone at a sports shop.

Fitness for a Lifetime!

How long should you exercise? Two years? Until you're twenty?

Answer: Always! Commit yourself to a lifetime of fitness. Once you begin a regular workout program, it will be easy. In fact, you won't feel quite right—almost sluggish—when you miss a week or two of workouts.

You're lucky—you're part of a new generation that knows how important exercise is to health. Take that information and run with it!

99

Source Notes

The Presidential Physical Fitness Award Program: Instructor's Guide. Washington, D.C.: U.S. Department of Health and Human Services, 1987.

Kraus-Weber tests for flexibility and strength, *American Health*, May 1987.

"Physical Education: A Performance Checklist." Washington, D.C.: President's Council on Physical Fitness and Sports.

Cycling has been an official Olympic Games sport since 1896. People also bicycle for fun, exercise, and transportation.

GLOSSARY

Accelerate To cause to move faster.

Achilles tendon The strong tendon, joining the muscles in the calf of the leg to the bone of the heel.

Aerobics Regular exercise that focuses on the increased use of oxygen, and strengthens the heart and lungs.

Agility The ability to move quickly with easy grace.

Appetite The desire to eat.

Artery A large blood vessel carrying blood away from the heart.

Biceps A large muscle at the front of the upper arm.

Blanche, blanching To become white or pale.

Blood The fluid that circulates in the heart and vessels of a vertebrate animal, carrying food and oxygen to, and waste away from, all parts of the body.

Caffeine A mild stimulant found in tea, coffee, cocoa, chocolate, and cola drinks (see "Nutrition").

Calf muscle The muscle located in the fleshy back part of the leg, below the knee.

Calisthenics Different exercises such as sit-ups, jumping jacks, and twist-and-turns, that don't usually require equipment and are done in one place.

Calorie The unit used to measure energy. All foods have an energy value, and exercising burns this energy.

Capillary Tiny blood vessels that connect the arteries to the veins.

Carotid artery The two chief vessels that pass up the neck to supply the head with blood.

Cholesterol A fatty substance produced by the body that comes from animal foods. Cholesterol aids in the production of cell membranes and hormones. Only very small amounts of cholesterol are needed by the body, but most people get too much (see "Nutrition").

Circulatory system The heart, blood, and blood vessels, which work together to carry blood and oxygen to and from all parts of the body.

Complex carbohydrates Also called starch. A nutrient and main source of energy for the body. Examples of complex carbohydrates are apples, potatoes, and whole-wheat breads (see "Nutrition").

Coordination The ability of the entire body to interact smoothly.

Diabetes A disease in which the body cannot properly break down sugar from food to use it as energy (see "Nutrition").

Digestion The body's process of breaking food down into simple substances so it can be absorbed into the bloodstream and carried to all parts of the body (see "Nutrition").

GLOSSARY

Digestive tract A series of organs that move food through the body, from the mouth to the anus.

Durable Long lasting.

Endurance The body's ability to handle stress for an extended period of time.

Equilibrium The ability to balance yourself.

Exhale To breathe out. To breathe in is "inhale."

Fat (1) Dietary fat is the fat found in food; it could be hidden inside a hot dog or be as obvious as butter or oil. Dietary fat is very high in calories, takes longer to digest than other nutrients, and is one of the nutrients we need very little of. People who eat a lot of fat are likely to have health problems such as obesity, cancer, and heart disease. (2) Body fat is the layer of cells beneath the skin. A little body fat is necessary to keep us warm and cushion our organs. Some people, however, eat too much dietary fat or high caloric sugary foods, and since the body stores extra calories, when it exceeds the number it needs for energy, there is a body fat excess (see "Nutrition").

Fatigue Feeling extremely tired and weary.

Flexibility The ability to bend, twist, and stretch the joints.

Frostbite The partial freezing of some part of the body.

Generic The general use of a name or term. Often, this means an overuse or misuse of a word or concept. Generic also refers to products without a brand name or trademark.

Glucose A natural sugar that occurs in many foods and is in the bloodstream.

Heart attack A serious condition that occurs when the heart doesn't receive enough blood, usually because a vessel is blocked.

High blood pressure, or hypertension. Blood pressure is the pressure of blood against the walls of the arteries. When a person exercises or becomes excited, the pressure goes up. The abnormal condition created when the blood pressure stays high all the time is called high blood pressure, or hypertension.

Hormones Body chemicals produced by different glands that move through the bloodstream. Hormones are the force behind most of the body's systems (see "Human Sexuality").

Hypothermia When the body temperature falls dangerously below normal.

Influenza, or flu. A disease usually spread by coughing or sneezing. Although very contagious, it is usually not serious. Sometimes, however, a new strain of flu appears and becomes an epidemic (affecting many people at one time).

GLOSSARY

Inhale To breathe in. To breathe out is "exhale".

Joint The point of contact between two parts of the skeleton with the parts that support and surround it. Examples of joints are the knee and elbow.

Ligament Tissue that connects two or more bones at a joint.

Menstruation The beginning of a female's monthly reproductive cycle, when blood and other tissues are discharged from the uterus, and out of the body (see "Human Sexuality").

Metabolism Cell activity within the body that changes food and oxygen into energy. The higher your metabolism, the more energy is burned.

Mononucleosis A sickness common among people ages 15–19. The virus is frequently passed through the saliva, giving it it's name of "the kissing disease." The symptoms of mononucleosis are sore throat, nauseau, chills, fever, and fatigue.

Muscles Body tissues that contract and move. With exercise, muscle tissue become firmer and can withstand more strain. If not used, the tissues break down.

Nonaerobics Exercise that isn't aerobic, and thus doesn't use as much oxygen as do aerobics. Usually this term refers to sports in which there is frequent rest between activity, such as golf or bowling.

Nutrients Substances in food that provide energy, build and repair cells, and regulate body processes. Some examples of nutrients are protein, carbohydrates, and fat (see "Nutrition").

Obesity The state of being extremely overweight.

Osteoporosis A disease characterized by weak bones caused by a lack of calcium, usually afflicting older women.

Overexert To put oneself through too much action or tiring effort.

Oxygen An invisible, odorless, tasteless gas ("air"). When you breathe, you take oxygen into your bloodstream, which then carries it to different parts of the body for fuel.

Perspiration A fluid secreted by the sweat glands of the skin. By releasing this mixture of water, salt, and body waste, the pores are able to cool off the body.

Physical Of, or relating to, the body.

President's Council on Physical Fitness and Sports A United States government agency created to promote exercise.

Protein An important nutrient, needed for building and replacing cells. Some examples of proteins are low-fat dairy products, beans, and chicken (see "Nutrition").

Psychological Mental; of or relating to the mind.

GLOSSARY

Pulse The regular beat of the heart.

Respiratory system The network involved when you inhale oxygen and exhale carbon dioxide.

Shin The front part of the leg, below the knee.

Speed The measure of how fast the body moves.

Stamina Staying power or endurance.

Strength The level at which your muscles are able to resist force.

Strenuous Very active; calling for energy and stamina.

Target heart rate The rate of your heartbeat when it is at 65–85 percent of its maximum level. If you don't exercise enough, you won't reach this level. If you push too hard, you may reach the highest rate, which places too great a strain on your heart.

Tendon A tough cord of tissue that connects a muscle with another body part that contracts when the muscles are worked.

Vein A vessel that carries blood to the heart.

Vessel A tube or canal in which blood is contained and circulated in the body.

Vigorous Carried out forcefully or energetically.

Whole grain A plant food in which none of the three parts of the kernel have been removed, like they have in white flour, white rice, and wheat bread. Some examples of whole grain foods are bran cereal, cornbread, oatmeal, whole-wheat flour, and brown rice (see "Nutrition").

HEALTH AND FITNESS ORGANIZATIONS

Still have some unanswered questions? Most of the organizations below have some published information they'll be happy to send you—if you just ask. Since your parents might not appreciate finding long-distance phone calls on their bills, it's probably best to write.

GENERAL ORGANIZATIONS

American Alliance for Health, Physical Education, Recreation, and Dance
1900 Association Drive
Reston, VA 22091
(703) 476-3488

American College of Sports Medicine
401 W. Michigan Street
Indianapolis, IN 46206
(317) 637-9200

American Running and Fitness Association
9310 Old Georgetown Road
Bethesda, MD 20814
(202) 667-4150

Association of Physical Fitness Centers
600 Jefferson Street
Suite 202
Rockville, MD 20852
(301) 656-5060

International Association of Physical Education and Sports For Girls and Women
50 Skyline Drive
Mankato, MN 56001
(507) 345-3665

International Physical Fitness Associations, Inc.
415 W. Court St.
Flint, MI 48503
(313) 239-2166

National Intramural-Recreational Sports Association
Gill Coliseum
Room 221
Oregon State University
Corvallis, OR 97331
(503) 754-2088

North American Youth Sports Institute
4985 Oak Garden Drive
Kernersville, NC 27284
(919) 784-4926

President's Council on Physical Fitness & Sports
Judiciary Plaza
450 Fifth Street NW
Suite 7103
Washington, DC 20001
(202) 272-3430

Women's Sports Foundation
342 Madison Avenue
Suite 728
New York, NY 10173
(212) 972-9170

AEROBICS AND DANCE

Aerobics and Fitness Association of America
15250 Ventura Boulevard
Suite 310
Sherman Oaks, CA 91403
(818) 905-0040

Institute for Aerobics Research
12330 Preston Road
Dallas, TX 75230
(800) 635-7050

International Dance Exercise Association
6190 Cornerstone Court East
Suite 204
San Diego, CA 92121
(619) 535-8979

International School of Aerobic Training
5555 Cloud Way
San Diego, CA 92111
(619) 571-8890

National Strength and Conditioning Association
916 O Street
P.O. Box 81416
Lincoln, NE 68501
(402) 472-3000

BASEBALL

Babe Ruth Baseball
P.O. Box 5000
1770 Brunswick Avenue
Trenton, NJ 08638
(609) 695-1434

Little League Baseball
P.O. Box 3485
Williamsport, PA 17701
(717) 326-1921

Pony Baseball
P.O. Box 225
Washington, PA 15301
(412) 225-1060

BASKETBALL

**National Amateur Basketball
   Association**
6832 West North Avenue
Suite 4A
Chicago, IL 60635
(312) 452-7570

BOWLING

Young American Bowling Alliance
5301 South 76th Street
Greendale, WI 53129
(414) 421-4700

BOXING

Knights Boxing Team
560 Campbell Hill
Marietta, GA 30060
(404) 426-7883

CYCLING

Bicycle Federation of America
1818 R Street NW
Washington, DC 20009
(202) 332-6986

FIGURE SKATING

**United States Figure Skating
   Association**
20 First Street
Colorado Springs, CO 80906
(303) 635-5200

FOOTBALL

Pop Warner Football
1315 Walnut Street
Suite 1632
Philadelphia, PA 19107
(215) 735-1450

GOLF

American Junior Golf Association
2415 Steeplechase Lane
Roswell, GA 30076
(404) 998-4653

Group Fore Golf Foundation
1056 Elwell Court
Palo Alto, CA 94303
(415) 967-1305

GYMNASTICS

United States Gymnastics Federation
201 S. Capitol
Suite 300
Indianapolis, IN 46225
(317) 237-5050

HOCKEY

**Amateur Hockey Association of the
   United States**
2997 Broadmoor Valley Road
Colorado Springs, CO 80906
(303) 576-4990

JUDO/KARATE

American Judo Association
2941 State Street, #2
Santa Barbara, CA 93105
(805) 569-0267

American Amateur Karate Federation
1930 Wilshire Boulevard
Suite 1208
Los Angeles, CA 90057
(213) 483-8261

INDEX